Sempre Susan

Sempre Susan

A MEMOIR OF SUSAN SONTAG

Sigrid Nunez

RIVERHEAD BOOKS *New York*

RIVERHEAD BOOKS
Published by the Penguin Group
Penguin Group (USA) LLC
375 Hudson Street, New York, New York 10014

USA • Canada • UK • Ireland • Australia • New Zealand • India • South Africa • China

penguin.com

A Penguin Random House Company

Previously published by Atlas & Co. Publishers in 2011
First Riverhead trade paperback edition: October 2014
Riverhead trade paperback ISBN: 978-1-59463-334-8

PRINTED IN THE UNITED STATES OF AMERICA

Book design by Tiffany Estreicher

While the author has made every effort to provide accurate telephone numbers and Internet
addresses at the time of publication, neither the author nor the publisher is responsible for errors,
or for changes that occur after publication. Further, the publisher does not have any control over and
does not assume any responsibility for author or third-party websites or their content.

Penguin is committed to publishing works of quality and integrity.
In that spirit, we are proud to offer this book to our readers;
however, the story, the experiences, and the words
are the author's alone.

Sempre Susan

I T WAS MY first time ever going to a writers' colony, and, for some reason I no longer recall, I had to postpone the date on which I was supposed to arrive. I was concerned that arriving late would be frowned on. But Susan insisted this was not a bad thing. "It's always good to start off anything by breaking a rule." For her, arriving late *was* the rule. "The only time I worry about being late is for a plane or for the opera." When people complained about always having to wait for her, she was unapologetic. "I figure, if people aren't smart enough to bring along something to read . . ." (But when certain people wised up and she ended up having to wait for them, she was not pleased.)

My own fastidious punctuality could get on her nerves.

Out to lunch with her one day, realizing I was going to be late getting back to work, I jumped up from the table, and she scoffed, "Sit down! You don't have to be there on the dot. Don't be so servile." *Servile* was one of her favorite words.

Exceptionalism. Was it really a good idea for the three of us—Susan, her son, myself—to share the same household? Shouldn't David and I get a place of our own? She said she saw no reason why we couldn't all go on living together, even if David and I were to have a child. She'd gladly support us all if she had to, she said. And when I expressed doubts: "Don't be so conventional. Who says we have to live like everyone else?"

(Once, on St. Mark's Place, she pointed out two eccentric-looking women, one middle-aged, the other elderly, both dressed like gypsies and with long, flowing gray hair. "Old bohemians," she said. And she added, jokingly, "Us in thirty years."

More than thirty years have passed, and she is dead, and there is no bohemia anymore.)

She was forty-three when we met, but she seemed very old to me. This was partly because I was twenty-five, and at that age anyone over forty seemed old to me. But it was also because she was recuperating from a radical mastectomy. (Break a rule: when hospital staff scolded her for refusing to do the recommended rehabilitation exercises, a sympathetic nurse whispered in her ear, "Happy Rockefeller wouldn't do them, either.") Her skin was sallow, and her hair—it would always bewilder me that so many people thought she bleached the white streak in her hair when it should have been obvious the streak was the only part that was its true color. (A hairdresser suggested that leaving one section undyed would look less artificial.) Chemotherapy had thinned much but not all of her extraordinarily thick, black hair, but the hair that grew back was mostly white or gray.

So, an odd thing: when we first met, she looked older than she would as I got to know her. As her health returned, she looked younger and younger, and when she decided to color her hair she looked younger still.

It was spring, 1976, almost a year after I'd finished my MFA at Columbia, and I was living on West 106th Street. Susan, who lived at the corner of 106th Street and Riverside Drive, had a pile of unanswered correspondence she had let accumulate during her illness and which she now wanted to get through. She asked some friends, the editors of *The New York Review of Books*, to recommend someone who might help her. I had worked as an editorial assistant at the *Review* between college and grad school. The editors knew that I could type and that I lived nearby, so they suggested that she call me. It was exactly the kind of odd job I was looking for then: the kind unlikely to interfere with my writing.

The first day I went to 340 Riverside Drive, it was sunny, and the apartment—a penthouse with many large windows—was blindingly bright. We worked in Susan's bedroom, I at her desk, typing on her massive IBM Selectric while she dictated, either pacing the room or lying on her bed. The room, like the rest of the apartment, was austerely furnished; the walls were white and bare. As she later explained, because this was where she worked, she wanted as much white space around her as possible, and she tried to keep the room as free as possible of books. I don't remember any pictures of family or friends (in fact, I can recall no such pictures on display anywhere in that apartment); instead, there were a few black-and-white photos (like the kind that came in publishers' publicity packets) of some of her literary heroes: Proust, Wilde, Artaud (a volume of whose selected writings she had just finished editing), Walter Benjamin. Elsewhere in the apartment there were a number of photographs of old movie stars, and stills from famous old black-and-white films. (These, as I recall, had previously decorated the lobby of the New Yorker Theater, the revival house at 88th Street and Broadway.)

4

She was wearing a loose turtleneck shirt, jeans, and Ho Chi Minh tire flip-flops, which I believe she had brought back from one of her trips to North Vietnam. Because of the cancer, she was trying to quit smoking (she would try and fail and try again, time after time). She went through a whole jar of corn nuts, washing them down with swigs from a plastic gallon jug of water.

The pile of letters was daunting; it would take many hours to get through, but what made our progress absurdly slow was that the phone kept ringing, and each time it rang she would pick up and chat (in some cases for quite some time) while I sat there, waiting, and, of course, listening, sometimes petting her son's large, attention-seeking malamute dog. Most of the callers were people whose names I knew. I gathered she was appalled at the way many people were responding to the news of her cancer. (Though I didn't know it yet, she was already working out ideas for what would become her essay "Illness as Metaphor.") I remember her describing cancer to one of her callers as "the imperial disease." I heard her say to several people that the recent deaths of Lionel Trilling and Hannah Arendt had left her feeling "orphaned." Fierce indignation as she reported someone saying of Trilling that it was no wonder he'd gotten cancer since he probably hadn't fucked his wife in years. ("And this was an *academic* speaking.") She hated to admit it, but she bravely did: one

5

of her own first thoughts when she'd been told she had cancer was "Did I not have enough sex?"

Once, it was her son who called. A year younger than I, David, who'd dropped out of Amherst, had recently returned to school and was now a sophomore at Princeton. He had a place to stay in Princeton, but most of the week he lived with his mother. His (soon to be our) bedroom was right next to hers.

—The work bored her. After we'd taken care of only a few letters, she suggested we break for lunch. I followed her to the other end of the apartment, passing through halls lined with books, and a dining area, where I admired a long, elegant wood table with matching wood benches (an old French farmhouse table, she informed me), and a framed vintage Olivetti poster (*"la rapidissima"*) hanging on the wall behind it. The dining table was usually covered with books and papers, and most meals were eaten in the kitchen, at a wood counter someone had painted dark blue.

I sat on a stool at the counter feeling very self-conscious while she heated up a can of Campbell's Cream of Mushroom soup. Add a can of milk and there was enough for two. It surprised me that she was so conversational. I was used to the hierarchical world of *The New York Review*, whose editors never made conversation with the staff. That day, I learned that the apartment's previous tenant had been her friend Jasper Johns; several years earlier, when

Johns had decided to move elsewhere, Susan had taken over the lease. Sadly, though, she didn't think she was going to be allowed to stay; the building's owner wanted that apartment for himself. It was obvious why Susan wanted to keep it: a large, two-bedroom penthouse apartment in a handsome prewar building—a terrific bargain at, as I recall, around 475 dollars a month. The enormous living room felt even bigger because there was so little in it (it even echoed slightly). But what she'd miss most, she said, was the view: the river, the sunsets. (That great view might have been even better from outdoors, but the terrace was a mess: it was where the dog did its business.) At the other end of the apartment from the two bedrooms was a much smaller room, once a maid's room, with half a bath. At the time, a friend of David's was sleeping there. After I moved in, it would be my study. ("You're the only one in this house with *two* rooms," Susan would say, hurt, accusing, when I told her that I was leaving "340.")

Over lunch, she asked me a lot of questions about what it was like to work for editors Robert Silvers and Barbara Epstein at *The New York Review*, and what it was like to study with Elizabeth Hardwick, who'd been one of my professors at Barnard and who was also on the editorial board of the *Review*. It was clear that these three people aroused Susan's keenest interest—fascination, even—and I would learn that their friendship and approval meant everything to her. All three had been among the *Review*'s founders, in 1963. Susan thought the *Review* was far superior to any other journal in the country—a "heroic" effort to elevate American intellectual life to the highest possible standards—and she was proud to have been writing for it from its very first issue. Her essays were edited by Silvers: "By far the best editor I've ever had." The best editor any writer *could* have, she would say. Like other contributors to the *Review*, she was awed by the grave respect he had for writers, by his perfectionism, and by the intense labor he put into revising articles for publication. He was one of the most intelligent and gifted persons she had ever met, she said—and probably the hardest-working, almost always to be found at his desk, seven days a week, including holidays, all day long and usually well into the night. His was precisely the kind of discipline and intellectual passion and scrupulosity that Susan admired most in other people, and he inspired in her the same reverence usually inspired in her only by the most serious writers and artists.

Her pride in writing for *The New York Review* was matched by her pride in having Farrar, Straus and Giroux as her book publisher. In fact, her longest and most intimate phone conversation that day was with Roger Straus, who, as head of FSG, had published Susan's first book thirteen years before, and who would go on to publish all her other books. It was not unusual for the two of them to talk at least once a day. At that time, Susan had no literary agent, and besides publishing her books, Straus took care of certain kinds of business that a publisher would not normally deal with, such as trying to place her short stories and articles with magazines. But theirs was not just a business relationship; they were old, good friends, they were each other's confidants, and Straus was involved in many aspects of Susan's nonwriting life, including the crisis of her illness and, when the time came, her search for a new apartment. Although David was already ten years old when Susan and Straus first met, Straus often referred to him as "probably my illegitimate son." Soon he would take David into the company, making him the editor of, among other authors, Susan herself.

The soup was not enough. She searched the fridge, which was mostly bare, but though it was not the season for corn there was a plastic-wrapped package of cobs. After we'd eaten the corn, she said, "Of course, I didn't want any of that. All I really wanted was a cigarette." I had just recently quit smoking myself, but once I moved in I would start up again. All three of us smoked, as did pretty much everyone who ever came to that apartment.

By the time I left that day, the sun was low over the Hudson but we'd accomplished very little. Susan asked me to come back in a few days. I remember thinking as I walked home how laid-back and open she'd been—much more like someone my own age than someone of my mother's generation. But she was always this way with young people, and there wasn't the usual generational distance between her and her son, either; her son, whom she'd started treating like an adult before he even reached high school, without ever appearing to doubt that this was how things should be. When I think of this now, I can't help thinking also of something Susan said often: how she remembered childhood as a time of complete boredom, and how she could not wait for it to be over. I have always had trouble understanding this (how could anyone's childhood—even a less than happy one—be described as "a total waste"?), but she had wanted David's childhood to be over as quickly as possible, too. (And as it turned out, he too would look back on his childhood as a miserable time, using the very phrase Susan often used in describing her own: a prison sentence. It was as if somehow she didn't really believe— or, perhaps, better to say, she saw no *value*—in childhood.

To David, she became "Susan" while he was still a boy, and his father, sociologist and cultural critic Philip Rieff, was "Philip"; David told me he could not imagine calling them Mom and Dad. And whenever Susan spoke to David about his father—whom she had married when she was a seventeen-year-old student at the University of Chicago and he a twenty-eight-year-old instructor, and whom she had divorced seven years later—she referred to him as

Philip as well. David rarely said "my mother" when speaking of her, and I would have felt strange saying "your mother." It was *sempre* Susan. (Once, in my first days working at *The New York Review*, Robert Silvers said, "Get me Susan on the phone." As I reached for the Rolodex, I said, "Susan who?" Barbara Epstein was there, too, and when she heard this she laughed. "*Susan who*," she repeated, shaking her head, and I understood that she was laughing at me.)

Names. Susan confessed that she had never been thrilled about having been given such a boring, common name. ("*You don't look like a Susan*," she would say, mimicking the many people who'd said this to her.) She bristled and sharply corrected anyone who called her Sue. She disliked shortened forms and nicknames in general, though she often called David (whom she had named after Michelangelo's statue) Dig.

In those years, neither mother nor son had any contact with father. But once, when the three of us were driving to Philadelphia, where Susan had been invited to speak, and where David's father now lived with his second wife, Susan addressed David from the backseat: "I think you should take Sigrid to meet Philip." And so, the next day, before we drove back to New York, we drove to Philip Rieff's house. Susan said she would wait in the car. We had given no warning of our visit, and when we rang there was no response.

But through a small glass pane in the front door, it was possible to peer just inside, where David pointed out his father's collection of canes.

I never did meet Philip Rieff. But when I read that he'd died, in 2006, I immediately thought of those canes and felt a pang.

I had read then only a little of Susan's writing. None of her work had been assigned in any course I'd taken in school, and I could remember her name coming up just once. A professor drew our attention to the fact that Philip Rieff, the editor of the texts of Freud's papers on our reading list, had been married to Susan Sontag, who, after their divorce, had written a book called *Against Interpretation*. Which, he said with a giggle, had always struck him as hilarious.

At that time there was a used-book store called Pomander on West 95th Street. There I found hardcover editions of the two novels, *The Benefactor* and *Death Kit*, and two essay collections, *Against Interpretation* and *Styles of Radical Will*, that Susan had published so far. (By then she had also made three films. Surely another reason she seemed so old to me was that she had already accomplished so much and had been famous since I was a girl.) As I was paying for the books, the store's owner said, "Ah, Susan Sontag, she comes in here all the time." (No doubt every time she caught a film at the old Thalia art house next door.) "But now she's very ill. She's dying."

I remember I did not take these last words seriously. I had just spent several hours with her. She did not seem "very ill." She did not act like a person who was dying. I knew that she had breast cancer, but I did not yet know all the facts. I did not know how advanced her case was, how sobering her prognosis. My father had died of cancer not that long before, but somehow I never saw Susan as being threatened in the same way. She might have seemed old to me, but she was twenty years younger than my father had been when he died. And when she did die, three decades later, although the news did not come as a surprise (I knew that she'd been gravely ill), it was a shock. The friend from whom I first heard the news said, "She was such a vital presence, and that she should have been felled in this way is very dismaying." I remember that the word *felled* appealed to me; I thought Susan would have liked it, too. I could not think of many other writers whose passing would have inspired such a response. (Immediately, though, there came to mind that fictional famous writer, news of whose death in Venice, we are told, is received by the world—despite the fact that he was an old man—with shock.) Though she was about to turn seventy-two when she died—though she was suffering from an almost certainly incurable form of leukemia—it was as if her life had been brutally cut short, as if she had been struck down in her prime. *Felled*.

I would discover there were many other people who'd felt the same shock as I had, and there were people who, in spite of Susan's age and the lethality of her disease, had firmly believed she would beat this cancer as she'd beaten cancers of the breast and the uterus earlier in life. And now it seems to me that to have been such a person, someone who struck others as too strong and tough, too *alive* to die, says something very wonderful about Susan. And it makes her own extreme behavior—as described by David after her death, her insistence on her exceptionalism, her refusal to admit that her case was hopeless, that death was not only inevitable, not only near, but *here*—seem, if no less delusional, perhaps a little more comprehensible.

I quickly read her four books, one after the other. I had an idea (prescient, as it turned out) that before long she was going to ask me which ones I'd read, and that the correct answer was *all of them*. And, like so many other readers of her work, I found the essays enthralling and the novels hard going.

At the time, I was in a swoon over Virginia Woolf. I was in awe of Professor Hardwick, who'd been not only my teacher but also the first professional writer I ever met, and about whom Susan herself would say, "She writes more beautiful sentences than any living American writer." Susan spoke dreamily at times of wanting to get "more Lizzie" into her own prose. The maker of shapely, beautifully cadenced sentences, Hardwick was also, according to Susan, "the queen of adjectives."

Susan's own writing was stirring, dramatic; it was dense with what we like to call "edgy" ideas, boldly stated. But her style—she didn't have a beautiful style. She didn't write beautiful sentences, and if there was something to admire in the novels, I wasn't getting it. This was disappointing, because a few years earlier I'd been enraptured by a story of hers in *The Atlantic Monthly*, "Project for a Trip to China": a hybrid work, as much essay as story, a work of imagination if not invention, a work that I'd clipped and saved (later it would be included in *I, etcetera*, her only collection of short fiction). It would be many years, though, before she would write a novel I could enjoy: *The Volcano Lover*, published in 1992.

Sometime in the mid-eighties, when she was struggling to write a memoir about a visit she had made as a teenager to the home of Thomas Mann (it would be published eventually as a short story called "Pilgrimage" in *The New Yorker*), she told me she had had a revelation about her fiction—about what it was missing. It had to do with detail, she said. Though a great admirer of Nabokov's prose, she had not followed his famous rule: caress the divine details. Part of the problem, she said, was that she didn't really notice details the way a writer like Nabokov did; or if she did notice them, she did not remember them later. For example, she could remember almost nothing specific about Thomas Mann's house that day. Which was very frustrating, she said, now that she wanted to tell that story.

If this was a weakness in her work, it was one she set out to correct with a vengeance when she sat down to write her next novel. *The Volcano Lover* is saturated with just the kind of sensuous, specific detail not to be found in her writing before.

I didn't keep a journal then—or if I did, it has long since vanished—so I can't say for sure exactly how many times I went to help Susan with her letters, but I think it was only three or four. And I believe it was the second time I went that I met her mother, who was visiting from out of town: a small, delicate-looking woman (her daughter looked hulking beside her) with chin-length hair dyed hard black. She looked like an aged flapper—like an old Louise Brooks. Red lipstick, and long red fingernails. I remember some kind of jewelry—I think rings. Do I remember or do I invent a cigarette holder? I definitely remember that she smoked. ("I wasn't going to, in front of Susan," she told me. "But when I saw David and everyone else lighting up . . .")

That day, when Susan and I were alone, she talked—in her open, confiding way—about her family. She told me she rarely saw her mother, that she'd left home when she was sixteen and from that time on she and her mother had had little to do with each other. When her mother first heard about the cancer, she'd sent Susan an electric blanket. Susan rolled her eyes and shrugged, as if this had been a clueless gesture. That day, I remember she talked about her mother frankly but without bitterness. But later, so much more would be said, and with so much feeling, that her mother would become almost mythical: a cold, selfish, narcissistic brute of a woman, who never showed Susan any affection, who never encouraged her gifted daughter, who appeared not even to have noticed she *had* a gifted daughter. "I would bring home these perfect report cards, and she'd sign them without saying a word. She never praised me, and she took no interest in my education at all."

The Bad Mother. The Dragon Lady. (Again: to David, she was Mildred, never Grandma.) She was stingy, too. "She never gave me a penny. When I went off to school, I was on my own. I could have starved to death." Everyone who knew Susan knew this story and how deep her resentment went.

17

She saw herself as a neglected, even an abandoned, child. Much of her care had been entrusted to another woman, Rosie, an Irish-American woman whom Susan described as illiterate, and who would come back into Susan's life after David was born. ("We joke that that's really why we're so much alike," Susan said. "Because we had the same nanny.")

Over and over we heard it: *My mother never cared what happened to me. My mother was never there for me.* It might as well have been yesterday. A wound that never healed.

She had a stepfather, whose surname she'd taken, and a younger sister. Though she did not speak of them with the same resentment with which she spoke of her mother, she explained that she was estranged from them as well. For she and they had nothing in common. She was the only intellectual, the only one with any passion for culture, the only one interested in politics. Her writing, her honors, her brilliant career—none of this meant much to her relatives, she said; her world was outer space to them.

Now I learned that "Project for a Trip to China" was—just as it had seemed—wholly autobiographical. (Unusual for her, she explained. She'd never been the kind of writer who wrote directly out of personal experience. In fact, "I'm *anti*-autobiographical," she said.)

Her father had died of tuberculosis when she was five. Her mother had waited several months to reveal that he was never coming back from China, where he'd been away on business, and she did so in a matter-of-fact way, as if it was nothing to fuss over. And then: "Boom," said Susan, "I had my first asthma attack." Her asthma would turn out to be troublesome enough that, following doctors' advice, the family would leave New York City, where Susan was born, and, after a brief stay in Miami, settle in Tucson. She would later suffer also from migraines and from periods of anemia. She remembered drinking daily glasses of the blood that her mother brought home from the butcher (an image I found very disturbing).

Because she barely remembered her father and was able to learn little about him, she had had to invent him. Naturally, she idealized him. It was beyond Susan (and not just her) how someone like average, incurious, unambitious Mildred could have produced her. She imagined her father, though he had not been highly educated, endowed with a good mind and other qualities she could admire. I thought she was right. I thought Jack Rosenblatt must have been quite a guy. She liked to think that, had he lived, he would have been a good father to her, the one family member she would have been able to relate to, proud of her achievements, able to share her enthusiasms. Her husband, of course, had been a terrible father. But she believed that her son would make not just a good but a *great* father. This was something she said all the time—as she said all the time that she believed that she had been a great mother. When she asked me once if I thought I'd make a good mother and I told the truth—I didn't know—she was put off. "How can you say such a thing about yourself?" It was as if I'd just confessed to being a bad person. She said she had never had any doubts about herself in this regard. In fact, not having had more children was one of her biggest regrets. She spoke of the "criminal" feeling she experienced every time she saw a baby or a young child. "I want to *kidnap* them!" Even the sight of a baby animal could wrench her. She once saw a baby elephant up close, she said, and was so overwhelmed "I sobbed and sobbed." (I supposed this must have had something to do with the fact that she and David had spent so much of his childhood apart. She had often left him in the care of other people, sometimes for long periods of time. Around his fifth birthday, for example, she had gone abroad and was not to see him again for well over a year.)

She told me that, when David was growing up, every time she did something that was the opposite of how her mother had done it (for example, encouraging him to go into her wallet anytime without asking and take whatever he wanted), she'd give herself points. "It felt so good to be able to say, I'm not like my mother." And indeed, she would always shower David with money.

I'm pretty sure it was the third time I went to 340 that I first met David. I was leaving the apartment just as he was coming home, and Susan briefly introduced us. I was surprised when, a day or so later, she called to ask me to come back—not the following week, as we'd planned, but rather that same afternoon. I said yes, of course, no problem. She'd sounded urgent. I didn't want to let her down.

When I arrived, Susan and David and the friend of David's who was living with them were all in the kitchen, drinking coffee. We sat around the counter awhile before Susan and I headed back to her bedroom to work. But we'd hardly gotten started when she threw up her hands and said, "I can't do this today, I'm just not in the mood. Why don't we go out for a pizza?" She meant the four of us, and so the four of us walked together to V&T's on Amsterdam Avenue.

I don't remember what we—or *they*, since I'm sure I hardly opened my mouth—talked about. I was too distracted. The truth was, I was in bad shape. I had just discovered that my boyfriend, with whom I'd been living for about two years, had started seeing someone else. He told me it had been a mistake, he wanted us to stay together—he'd give up the other woman—but I had strong doubts about this. First of all, I knew his history. He had a pat-

21

tern: in the middle of a relationship with one woman, he would start seeing someone else. After much zigzagging, he'd always end up with the second woman. So I didn't have much hope for our future, and besides, I wasn't sure I still wanted him. At the time, both he and the new girlfriend were working at *The New York Review*, where the affair was an open secret. I didn't want Susan to hear about it. What I didn't know was that she'd already heard about it. That was why she'd called. That was why we were in the pizzeria.

It turned out that the last time I'd been to 340, after Susan had introduced David and me and I had gone home, he had asked her if I had a boyfriend and she'd told him yes. But then almost immediately she heard from one of her friends at the *Review* that that relationship was probably over. She encouraged David to call me. He was shy. She was not.

The way it fell out in the next couple of weeks was this: I moved out of the apartment where I'd been living with my boyfriend and sublet a room in an apartment nearby, which two recent college graduates were already sharing. My plan was to stay there through the summer and then find a place of my own. My boyfriend continued to see the other woman, who soon moved in with him. I started dating David. Susan started dating Joseph Brodsky.

Joseph Brodsky had only recently settled in the United

States—he would become an American citizen the following year—having lived first in different European cities after being expelled from his homeland, Soviet Russia, in 1972. He was only thirty-six, but a hard life that had included near starvation during the German siege of Leningrad and a year and a half of compulsory farm labor (the part of a five-year sentence for "social parasitism" that he served in exile in northern Russia before the sentence was commuted), heavy smoking, and heart disease had aged him. He was mostly bald, he was missing teeth, and he had a paunch. He wore the same soiled, baggy clothes every day. But to Susan he was intensely romantic. This was the beginning of a friendship that would last until his death in 1996, and in those early days she was smitten with him. Susan was one of those literary Americans for whom European writers would always be superior to native ones and for whom there was something particularly exalted and seductive about a Russian writer, above all a Russian poet. Joseph Brodsky came with laudations from, among others, W. H. Auden and Anna Akhmatova. He was a hero, too. A martyr, even: a writer who had been made to suffer like a criminal for his art. And everyone knew he was going to win the Nobel Prize. Susan was at his feet. She saw flashes of genius in every passing remark, in the puns he was forever trying out ("Muerto Rico"), and in his casual quips ("If you want to be quoted, don't quote"). She indulged his long-winded Tolstoy bashing (he saw Tolstoy, "in no way equal to Dostoevsky," as a kind of highbrow Margaret Mitchell who had helped prepare the way for socialist realism) and his weirder literary judgments (Nabokov's writing was "too marinated"). She could forgive him his crudenesses (the young women of Mount Holyoke, where he taught, were "mounties"; gay men tilted their chins in a way that was "Greek asking").

"Now that I've gotten through this," said Susan, meaning her breast cancer (though at the time she was still undergoing treatment), "I want two things: I want to work and I want to have fun." Joseph was fun. He had an adorable, closed-lipped, almost whimpering kind of laugh, and he laughed a lot. He had been the victim of brutes, but he remained tenderhearted. He was loud about his opinion that poets were a superior class of human being and that he himself ranked among the best world poets, but he was not a snob or a preener. He was generous and naturally affectionate, he liked a good time—a good time was better when there were many people to share it—and he had a prankish, boyish sense of humor. He loved cats, and sometimes for a greeting he would meow. David had a car then, and I remember the four of us driving around Manhattan, four cigarettes going, the car filled with smoke and Joseph's deep, rumbling voice and funny, high-pitched laugh.

He wanted to write essays—not in his native Russian

but in the English he had taught himself. (He had started writing some poems in English as well.) He would write, like Susan, for *The New York Review*. In those early *Review* essays, Susan saw the usual marks of genius, but she saw weaknesses as well. He seemed sincerely eager to know her opinion, but she was torn. She wanted to be honest— believed she had a duty to be honest—but she did not know how he would take it. In the end, she decided he would not take it well. She could not criticize, she could only praise. But it sat on her conscience. She once tried to get me to be her mouthpiece ("It might be easier if he thinks it comes from you"), but I refused.

About *her* feelings, he was not so careful. Once, trying to explain why she would have preferred to stop writing criticism altogether and write only fiction (her chronic lament), she said, "I'm tired of working so hard. I want to *sing!*" Joseph, who had read some of her fiction, replied admonishingly, "Susan, you have to know, it is given to very few people to sing." (On the other hand, I remember that, although it was in the realist style that both he and Susan generally disparaged, he raved about a Jean Stafford story, "An Influx of Poets," when it came out in *The New Yorker*.)

He admonished Susan also for wanting to own so many books. The only proper thing to do with a book once you'd read it was to give it away.

"Susan, Susan, wait now, shut up, please, *I* am talking!" He always had to be the center of attention, the one doing most of the talking, and though he was always a pleasure to hear, I was often glad after we'd said good-bye and I could listen, uninterrupted, to what Susan had to say, which—for me, anyway—usually turned out to be more articulate and more enlightening. There were many things—movies, for example—that she knew more about than he.

Do I even need to say what an enormous privilege it was to hear them both? Looking back, I only wish that I could feel more joy—or, at least, that I could find a way of remembering that is not so painful.

> *. . . silence is the presence*
> *of farewells in our greetings as we touch.*

I had read the English translations of Joseph's poetry that had been published in 1973, with a foreword by Auden and dedicated to Auden's memory (he had died that same year). The poem that I recall causing the most excitement at 340 was "Elegy for John Donne." But it was this line, from canto 10 of "Gorbunov and Gorchakov," that haunted me. It haunts me still.

In those days Susan and David's favorite meal was sushi (a food they introduced me to), and eating out with one or both of them usually meant going to either of two

Japanese restaurants on Columbus Avenue or to a slightly fancier one in a certain midtown hotel.

With Joseph, though, it had to be Chinatown. I remember him on one particular night, a piece of sea cucumber dangling from his chopsticks, beaming at everyone around the table. "Aren't we happy?" he said, then turned to give Susan a kiss.

That night, sometime after we dropped him off at Morton Street, where he lived, he had his first heart attack.

I spent very little time in the room I was renting, but toward the end of the summer (during most of which Susan was away, at her second home, in Paris), I did find a new apartment. It was on a bad block, one of the many bad blocks to be found on the then half-slummy Upper West Side. I hadn't even moved in all my stuff when I was robbed. Neighbors informed me that the thief was the super and that I had not been his first victim. I confronted the super, who denied the crime while looking guilty—and mean— as hell. I complained to the landlord, who would not get involved. Change the locks if you're so suspicious, he told me wearily. The super seemed to me not only dishonest but a little psychotic, coolly entering apartments to rob tenants, leaving a window open to make it look as if the thief had come in that way (in the case of my apartment, the thief would have had to know how to fly). I was afraid to live there now. And in fact, I never did.

WHY WAS I going to a writers' colony, anyway? Susan wanted to know. She herself would never do that. If she was going to hole up and work for a spell, let it be in a hotel. She'd done that a couple of times and loved it, ordering sandwiches and coffee from room service and working feverishly. But to be secluded in some rural retreat just sounded grim. And what sort of inspiration was to be found in the country? Had I never read Plato? (Socrates to Phaedrus: "I'm a lover of learning, and trees and open country won't teach me anything.")

I never knew anyone who was more appreciative than Susan was of the beautiful in art and in human physical appearance—"I'm a beauty freak" was something she said all the time—and yet I never knew anyone less moved by the beauties of nature. To her, it could not have been more obvious: art was superior to nature as the city was superior to the country. Why would anyone want to leave Manhattan—"capital of the twentieth century," as she loved to say—for a month in the woods?

When I said I could easily imagine moving to the country, maybe not right then but when I was older, she was appalled. "That sounds like *retiring.*" The very word made her ill.

Because it was where her parents lived, she sometimes had to fly to Hawaii. When I said I was dying to visit America's most beautiful state, she was baffled. "But it's totally boring." Curiosity was a supreme virtue in her book, and she herself was endlessly curious—but not about the natural world. Though she often spoke admiringly of the view from her apartment, I never knew her to cross the street to go into Riverside Park.

Once, when we were walking together on a campus outside the city, a chipmunk zipped across our path and dove into a hole at the base of an oak tree. "Oh, look at that," she said. "Just like Walt Disney."

Another time, I showed her a story I was working on in which a dragonfly appeared. "What's that? Something you made up?" When I started to describe what a dragonfly was, she cut me off. "Never mind." It wasn't important; it was boring.

Boring, like *servile*, was one of her favorite words. Another was *exemplary*. Also, *serious*. "You can tell how serious people are by looking at their books." She meant not only what books they had on their shelves, but how the books were arranged. At that time she had about six thousand books, perhaps a third of the number she would eventually own. Because of her, I arranged my own books

SIGRID NUNEZ

by subject and in chronological rather than alphabetical order. I wanted to be serious.

"It *is* harder for a woman," she acknowledged. Meaning: to be serious, to take herself seriously, to get others to take her seriously. *She* had put her foot down while still a child. Let gender get in her way? Not on your life! But most women were too timid. Most women were afraid to assert themselves, afraid of looking too smart, too ambitious, too confident. They were afraid of being unladylike. They did not want to be seen as hard or cold or self-centered or arrogant. They were afraid of looking masculine. Rule number one was to get over all that.

Here is one of my favorite Susan Sontag stories.

It was sometime in the sixties, after she'd become a Farrar, Straus and Giroux author, and she was invited to a dinner party at the Strauses' Upper East Side town house. Back then, it was the custom chez Straus for the guests to separate after dinner, the men repairing to one room, the women to another. For a moment Susan was puzzled. Then it hit her. Without a word to the hostess, she stalked off to join the men.

Dorothea Straus told the story gleefully years later: "And that was that! Susan broke the tradition, and we never split up after dinner again."

She was certainly not afraid of looking masculine. And she was impatient with other women for not being more

30

like her. For not being able to leave the women's room and go join the men.

She always wore pants (usually jeans) and low-heeled shoes (usually sneakers), and she refused to carry a purse. The attachment of women to purses perplexed her. She made fun of me for taking mine everywhere. Where had women gotten the idea they'd be lost without one? Men didn't carry purses, hadn't I noticed? Why did women *burden* themselves? Why not instead always wear clothes with pockets large enough to hold keys, wallet, and cigarettes, as men did?

(She had to wear a skirt, though, if she wished to attend the Richard Wagner Festival in Bayreuth. For Wagner, Susan would dress like a lady. And, to go with that long, black, pleated silk skirt, which she bought in Paris, she had to wear stockings and heels. Back in New York, in a spirit of fun, she wore the outfit again, to a restaurant dinner party given by the Strauses. She vamped for us, and we all agreed the effect was very strange, even kinky.)

Though she had always been praised for her looks, she never struck me as vain. If I had to, I'd bet that, of all the many compliments she received, her favorite was from Pete Hamill: "possessed of the most intelligent face of her generation." (At any rate, shortly after he paid it—reporting on a memorial service for Robert Lowell in 1977—he and she went out together.) Her own judgment was mixed:

"Some days I look in the mirror and think, Hey, I'm really good-looking." Other days, her heart sank.

"I've always had a couple of features everyone finds unattractive," she said. Bags under her eyes, and what everyone now calls "cankles." Also, she bit her nails. She was self-conscious about the stretch marks pregnancy had given her, and though the loss of a breast hardly seemed too high a price to pay for survival, it was not something she, any more than any other woman, could take in stride. She refused, however, to be "ashamed." She would hike up her T-shirt to show her scar. "Isn't it amazing? I thought it would be hideous, but in fact it's really just like an erasure." Which was exactly so. She was not shy about exposing her chest to men, or to people she had just met. She thought everyone should be curious and able to look without flinching. (She hated squeamishness in people, and I can recall her taunting a fellow diner for blanching at a Thai dish that included pigs' ears. Pointing to a piece of pork on his plate, she said, "And what part of the piggy do you suppose this is?") She had considered, but in the end decided against, breast reconstruction. But when a friend expressed support for this decision, saying that, after all, Susan was no longer a young woman, she flared up. "I don't want to think like that. Like, my life—my sex life—is all behind me." (In fact, she didn't want age ever to be a factor in anything. She may have been in a big hurry to leave childhood, but she wished to live her entire life as if exempt from the realities of getting older.)

She said, "Here's a big difference between you and me. You wear makeup and you dress in a certain way that's meant to draw attention and help people find you attractive. But I won't do anything to draw attention to my looks. If someone wants to, they can take a closer look and maybe they'll discover I'm attractive. But I'm not going to do anything to help them." Mine was the typical female way, hers was the way of most men.

No makeup, but, as we know, she dyed her hair. And she wore cologne. Men's cologne: Dior Homme.

And, like most women, she fretted about her weight, which greatly fluctuated, depending on how much she was smoking, or how much she was writing, which, if a lot, usually meant she was also taking amphetamines. After forty, she was more often overweight than not. And, like so many women, she had her fad diet: skip six meals and lose six pounds. Not that this was easy. Susan loved to eat. (In fact, the thing we two probably had most in common was an embarrassing one: a voracious appetite.)

But she was happy with her height. Once, at a conference on feminism, she was moved to envy by Germaine Greer. "She was the only woman in the room who was taller than me." (The artist Saul Steinberg once strangely insisted that Susan was in fact not a true tall person like her son but rather two short people, one on top of the other.) In general, though, other women's physical attractions did not inspire envy in Susan.

She never exercised—she had never been in shape in her life—but, so long as the weather was warm, and so long as she was in a city, she enjoyed walking. She had a slow, loose, somewhat flat-footed stride, not graceful, but not unattractive. When she walked she held her chin high, and she often hooked her thumbs in the waistband or the pockets of her jeans.

She wore lots of black, though it was not her best color. With her olive skin, she looked better in white, rose, blue. I thought she should wear colors that made her look softer. I didn't see why she had to look so tough. She could look like a prison matron at times.

She told me that she had had to be taught how to dress. She had come of age knowing nothing about clothing or style. "I was Miss Dowdy. I thought polyester was just fine."

She often shook or tossed her hair, and combing it out of her face with the fingers of one hand was one of her most characteristic gestures. Once it appeared, I didn't like the white streak, which to me looked anything but natural.

. . .

Much has been made—not least by Susan herself—of her "morbid" (her word) obsession with beauty. But it should be said that her taste in physical beauty, like her taste in most other things, was very broad. She saw beauty in all types, and in many men and women whom others did not find remarkable at all. If a person had even one striking feature— a good body, for example, or big blue eyes—that person was "to die for." How was one to take, for example, her account of the people she had observed in North Vietnam, where "every other person looked like a movie star"? I saw it as part of her habit of exaggeration: every work of art she liked was a masterpiece, every artist who moved her was a genius, every man or woman who acted bravely was a hero, and around every corner came Helen or Adonis.

Sometimes she bemoaned the hold a person's looks could have on her. In the case of one ex-lover, whom Susan had come to loathe in the way you can loathe only someone you once madly adored, she declared that there was only one reason this woman continued to make her suffer each time Susan saw her. "If she went around wearing a paper bag over her head, I'd be just fine." When others failed to see such fearsome beauty in this particular woman, Susan thought they must be blind.

Susceptible is the word that comes to me. She was susceptible. "If I'm close to someone, even if it's just a friend,

I always feel some sexual attraction to that person." She often ended up sleeping with friends.

Though she would always revere Elizabeth Hardwick's work, she thought Hardwick was yet another woman fettered by her femininity ("I have always, all of my life, been looking for help from a man," Hardwick once wrote), in this case a particularly pungent Southern brand of it. (On the other hand, in a conversation about women writers I once had with Hardwick, when I mentioned Susan she said, "She's not really a woman.")

Susan thought Virginia Woolf was a genius, but to hold her above all other literary idols, as I did then, struck her as callow, predictable. Besides, something about Woolf— something I think had everything to do with Woolf's mental and physical illnesses (her weaknesses, in other words)—made Susan queasy. The first volume of Woolf's letters had recently come out, and Susan said she could not read them. She was put off by the many intimate letters to Woolf's beloved older friend, Violet Dickinson, the silly endearments and girlish prattle, and Woolf's habit of presenting herself as a cute little animal. Susan hated childish language of any kind and always boasted that she had never spoken baby talk with her son when he was little.

But, for my birthday, she gave me a volume of the two holograph drafts of *The Waves*.

She was suspicious of women with menstrual complaints. She herself had always taken her periods in stride, and she thought that a lot of women must be exaggerating the inconveniences and discomforts of theirs. Or they were buying into old myths about the delicacy and vulnerability of the female body. In fact, she suspected that many people exaggerated or overreacted to both physical and emotional pain, an attitude that no doubt owed much to her having had cancer and having stoically withstood radical surgery and chemotherapy. In my case, diagnosis was simple: "You're neurasthenic." David's last girlfriend had had severe dysmenorrhea, and Susan was starting to worry. "I don't want David to think all women are like this."

Once, before leaving the house, she saw me slip some tampons into my purse, and this irked her. The purse was bad enough, and now: "We're just going out for a couple of hours, you don't need all those tampons!" (Nor did she see why a person needed to own so many pairs of underwear. I should learn from her: own just one or two pairs and wash out the ones you wore during the day before going to bed each night.)

Seeing me curled up in her son's lap, she fixed me with a cool I've-got-your-number look and lisped mockingly, "The little girl and her *big man*."

. . .

She was a feminist, but she was often critical of her feminist sisters and of much of the rhetoric of feminism for being naïve, sentimental, and anti-intellectual. And she could be hostile to those who complained about being underrepresented in the arts or banned from the canon, ungently reminding them that the canon (or art, or genius, or talent, or literature) was not an equal opportunity employer.

She was a feminist who found most women wanting. There was a certain friend she saw regularly, a brilliant man whom she loved to hear talk and whom, though he was married, she usually saw alone. Those times when his wife did come along, though, were inevitably disappointing. With his wife there, Susan complained, the conversation of this brilliant and intellectually stimulating man somehow became boring.

She was exasperated to find that the company of even very intelligent women was usually not as interesting as that of intelligent men.

———

THAT FALL, SHORTLY after I moved into 340, and a year after she had been diagnosed with cancer, Susan was back in the hospital. Something had shown up on one of the medical tests that she routinely underwent, along with chemotherapy, and her doctors were concerned. To find out more, they would have to operate. Though in the end this would turn out to have been just a scare, it threw Susan and everyone around her into turmoil.

Nicole Stéphane, the woman with whom Susan had been romantically involved for several years, and with whom she shared a home in Paris, flew to New York. She arrived a few days before the surgery and stayed on for about a week after Susan was discharged from the hospital.

I was excited to meet Nicole. I was a big fan of *Les Enfants Terribles*, the 1950 Jean-Pierre Melville film in which she had starred when she was in her twenties—a hypnotizing performance that had received much applause. But soon after making the film, she gave up acting—partly because of a serious car accident, but also, according to Susan, because, though extremely gifted, she did not have the right temperament to be a movie star. Susan clearly admired her for having been able to walk away from fame—and for something else even more: during World War II, Nicole, though hardly more than a girl at the time, had been part of the Resistance.

Rather than continue to act in films, Nicole would produce them, including Susan's *Promised Lands*, a documentary set in Israel around the end of the 1973 Yom Kippur War. When I met Nicole she was engaged in a byzantine effort to produce a film version of Proust's *In Search of*

Lost Time, a seemingly cursed project with which she would struggle for years to come.

Nicole was ten years older than Susan, and her affection had a strong maternal side. She saw it as her duty to take care of Susan, which seemed to come down mostly to feeding her. In fact, whenever she came to New York, she spent most of her time food shopping (she liked Zabar's and, across town, Lobel's meat market on the Upper East Side) and preparing delicious meals. But it seemed none of this could be accomplished without drama. Often when she was busy in the kitchen she could be heard muttering and swearing in French and slamming things around. Among other frustrations, Upper West Side kitchens in those days were overrun with roaches. But on this particular visit, there was no end of things that could offend Nicole, and at least once a day she broke into tears or exploded in rage, or both.

Like the good actor she was, she convinced me that she was enchanted to meet me and only too happy to welcome me into the family, though it was not so. She had a troubled history with David, and had always taken Susan's side in the many conflicts between mother and son. Now it disgusted—but hardly surprised—her that he'd found himself a girlfriend who didn't even know how to boil an egg. She misunderstood a remark someone let fall (Nicole's English was weak) and then could not be unconvinced of the notion that I was on some kind of superdangerous birth control pill (in fact, I wasn't on the pill at all) that could result in my one day giving birth to a freak. In other words, I was reckless as well as incompetent. And the way I *hung* on David, even in public. Like a tramp. It made him sloth-ful, she said.

All these charges against me—and more—she voiced to others close to the household, who repeated her words to me, as she probably knew they would, while to my face she remained . . . enchanted.

Sometimes she would take a black Magic Marker and write "Susan Only!" on various items in the fridge.

When she was away from Susan she worried about her, above all about what she was eating. (Even before Susan became ill, Nicole had been known to call all the way from Paris to the local bodega and order groceries to be deliv-ered to Susan's door.) How could she ever relax, knowing Susan was in the hands of a pair of selfish good-for-nothings like David and me?

It was true that as soon as Nicole was gone we'd return to our habit of eating out, or eating takeout, all the time. I can't recall any real cooking being done at 340 unless it was by Nicole or some other visitor. No entertaining, not even on holidays. If there was a guest, he or she would be offered a cup of Café Bustelo (never any kind of alcohol) or might be invited to join us for a frozen dinner or a bowl of canned soup. David was addicted to junk food and could go a whole day eating nothing but chips. Until she started worrying about carcinogens in nitrates, Susan had been in the habit of making a meal out of a package of bacon. Every once in a while one of us would throw some lamb chops or chicken wings into a pan and cook the hell out of them. Once, I bought a pork roast at the supermarket and Susan showed me how to cook it Cuban style, like her Cuban-born former lover, playwright Maria Irene Fornés, used to do, with slivers of garlic embedded in cuts in the meat.

I remember one day, right after I'd moved in, the three of us sitting around feeling terribly hungry and terribly lazy and wondering what on earth we could eat. I offered to go out and get some canned tuna fish and a loaf of bread and make us sandwiches, which we could eat with chips. Susan and David exchanged a look. "So goy?" said Susan. So I went and got us some takeout from the Cuban-Chinese diner at 109th Street and Broadway instead.

As Susan kept trying to assure me, Nicole's bad mood during her visit was hardly my fault. In fact, their relationship, always fraught with conflict, had been slowly and messily unraveling. That summer in Paris they had fought nonstop. They would remain friends (Nicole would outlive Susan by less than three years, dying at the age of eighty-three in 2007), but the life they had shared as a couple was coming to an end.

Not long after Nicole's visit, the woman who had been Susan's lover before Nicole, an Italian woman named Carlotta, who lived in Rome, came to stay. She and I had no trouble getting along, but, though easygoing compared with Nicole, Carlotta was prone to depressions that left her nearly catatonic, and which turned Susan off.

In fact, in spite of having just dodged a bullet, Susan was depressed herself. On the one hand, it was of course a very good thing that both Nicole and Carlotta would come such a long way to be with Susan in her time of need. On the other, it hardly lifted the spirits to be reminded of relationships that had begun in romance and passion but were now dead. Susan was alone, and she did not want to be alone. She wanted to be in love. (She believed in love, and when she fell she fell *hard*, and in her feelings there was an element of terror.) She wanted to be married. It would torment her all her life that no relationship of hers, no matter how deeply and truly she cared for the other, had endured. The affair with Joseph Brodsky had been short-lived, and he had not let her down gently. In fact, he had been mean. ("Mean, smart men and silly women," she once said drolly, "seem to be my fate.") Though she always had much to deplore about her marriage to Philip Rieff, as time passed she would reminisce wistfully about their closeness: how he so hated to be separated from her that he'd even follow her into the bathroom. "He couldn't interrupt the conversation even to let me pee." And they seemed never to run out of conversation. It was this kind of intimacy that she craved and that she feared she would never know again. She was working—mainly on the last two of the series of essays on photography she'd begun writing in 1973—but she was not having fun.

———

OVER THE YEARS, I have met or learned about a surprising number of people who said it was reading Susan Sontag when they were young that had made them want to be writers. Although this was not true of me, her influence on how I think and write has been profound. By the time I got to know her, I was already out of school, but I'd been a mostly indifferent, highly distracted student, and the gaps in my knowledge were huge. Though she hadn't grown up in New York, she was far more of a New Yorker than I, who'd always lived there, and you could have had no better guide to the city's cultural life than she. Small wonder I considered meeting her one of the luckiest strokes of my life. It's quite possible that, in time, I'd have discovered on my own such writers as John Berger and Walter Benjamin and E. M. Cioran and Simone Weil. But the fact remains, I learned about them first from her. Though I'm sure she was often dismayed to discover what I hadn't read, how much I didn't know, she did not make me feel ashamed. Among other things, she understood what it was like to come from a place where there were few books and no intellectual spirit or guidance. She said, "You and I didn't have what David's been able to take for granted from birth."

After I published a memorial essay in which I had written that Susan was not a snob, I heard some outraged responses: everyone knew she was a *terrible* snob! What I meant was that she did not believe a person must be lacking in any worthy quality simply because of his or her roots, no matter how primitive or deprived; she was not a class snob. She was the kind of person who noticed that the uneducated young woman who cleaned her house for a time had "beautiful, naturally aristocratic manners." On the other hand, she never pretended that a person's success did not depend—and to no small extent, either—on being connected (about a woman who'd asked her for a letter of recommendation for a certain fellowship, she said, "She'll never, ever get it—not because her work isn't good enough, she just doesn't know the right people"), or that she didn't know what Pascal meant when he said that being wellborn can save a man thirty years.

In fact, the ways of the wellborn (a significant number of whom would always chase after Susan) were a never-ending source of fascination to her. She came home from a dinner party once with this story: one of the guests, a woman from a well-known wealthy family, had fallen asleep and, while the others drank their coffee, sat with her head thrown back and her mouth open, snoring. Susan told this story in tones of awe. "Now, that's class assurance." And there was another awe-inspiring story, about the young patron of a theatrical production who had invited her and a large group of people to a restaurant for drinks after a preview performance. When the maître d' said they could not have a table if all they were going to order was drinks, the young man told him, "No problem. Just bring us our drinks, and you can charge us for dinner." (Meaning, of course, charge *him*.) In an airport once, struck by the beautiful skin of a man sitting near her, Susan made a bet with herself. And sure enough, she reported later, when it was time to board, the man turned out to be flying first class.

This kind of observation was very common to her, but it did not make her a snob. She could not have cared less if a person came from a "good" or a "bad" family; she knew the distinction was specious. Wherever you were from, what really mattered to her was how smart you were—for, needless to say, she *was* an elitist. And if you had taste and were intellectually curious, you didn't even have to be that smart. And if you were gorgeous, you didn't have to be smart at all. And though she could get quite riled at a bookstore clerk who didn't recognize her name, it was okay when a New York City Ballet dancer to whom she was introduced said, "And what do *you* do?" (Susan who?)

The gaps in my knowledge didn't really surprise her. She had a low opinion of American education and of American culture in general, and she took it for granted that I could learn more in a year at 340 than I had in six years at an American university. She was a natural mentor. She didn't have what would be called exactly protégés (except, I suppose, for David), but you could not live with Susan or spend any significant time with her and avoid being mentored. Even someone who met her only once was likely to go away with a reading list. She was naturally didactic and moralistic; she wanted to be an influence, a model, *exemplary*. She wanted to improve the minds and refine the tastes of other people, to tell people things they didn't know (in some cases, things they didn't even want to know but that she insisted they damn well ought to). But if educating others was an obligation, it was also loads of fun. She was the opposite of Thomas Bernhard's comic "possessive thinker," who feeds on the fantasy that every book or painting or piece of music he loves has been created solely for and belongs solely to him, and whose "art selfishness" makes the thought of anyone else enjoying or appreciating the works of genius he reveres intolerable. She wanted her passions to be shared by all, and to respond with equal intensity to any work she loved was to give her one of her biggest pleasures.

47

SIGRID NUNEZ

Some of her enthusiasms mystified me. As we sat in the
theater, sharing a giant chocolate bar, I kept wondering
why she had wanted to see a double feature of old Katha-
rine Hepburn movies, both of which she said she'd already
seen more than twenty times. Of course, she was *besotted*
(another favorite word) with moviegoing—in the way,
perhaps, that only someone who never watches television
can be. (We know this now: if one size screen doesn't
addict you, another one will.) We went to the movies all the
time. Ozu, Kurosawa, Godard, Bresson, Resnais—each of
these names is linked in my mind with her own. It was with
her that I first learned how much more exciting a movie
is when watched from a seat close up to the screen.
Because of her, I still always sit in the front of the theater,
I still resist watching any movie on television, and I
have never been able to bring myself to rent movie videos
or DVDs.

Among living American writers, she admired, besides
Hardwick, Donald Barthelme, William Gass, Leonard
Michaels, Joan Didion, Grace Paley. But she had no more
use for most contemporary American fiction (which, as she
lamented, usually fell into either of two superficial catego-
ries: passé suburban realism or "Bloomingdale's nihilism")
than she did for most contemporary American film. In her

view, the last first-rate American novel had been *Light in August*, by Faulkner (a writer she respected but did not love). Of course, Philip Roth and John Updike were good writers, but she could summon no enthusiasm for the things they wrote about. Later, she would not find the influence of Raymond Carver on American fiction something to cheer. It wasn't at all that she was against minimalism, she said; she just couldn't be thrilled about a writer "who writes the same way he talks."

What thrilled her instead was the work of certain Europeans, for example Italo Calvino, Bohumil Hrabal, Peter Handke, Stanislaw Lem. They, along with Latin American writers such as Jorge Luis Borges and Julio Cortázar, were creating far more daring and original work than her less ambitious fellow Americans. She liked to describe all highly inventive form- or genre-bending writing as science fiction, in contrast to banal contemporary American realism. It was this kind of literature that she thought a writer should aspire to, and that she aspired to, and that she believed would continue to matter.

I cannot recall a single book she recommended that I was not glad to have read. One of the last times I saw her, it was W. G. Sebald's *The Emigrants* that she went on and on about. *The Emigrants* would become one of my favorite books, and Sebald would become an important influence— and again, I heard about him first from her.

I would have read anything that she told me to read. When it came to writing, though, it was a different matter.

It took me weeks to get up the courage to show her any of my work, though she, in her typical way, kept prodding. ("I'm dying of curiosity!") The story I finally gave her was not a story at all but the sort of thing Flannery O'Connor (another major American writer Susan did not love) had in mind when she complained about beginning fiction writers being "concerned primarily with unfleshed ideas and emotions." Susan saw the problem at once. "You need an agon," she said. And then, of course, she had to explain to me what that meant.

At other times she cautioned me against being too explicit, and she said I should try to write more elliptically and streamline the prose to get it moving at a faster clip. ("If there's one thing modernism has taught us, it's that speed is everything.") Describing an evening as sultry, she told me, was as bad as describing someone as having distinguished gray hair.

Other than this, though, I remember very little that she said about anything I ever showed her that was helpful. Most of the problem lay with me: I was like a lot of the students I would end up teaching. It's not criticism many young writers want, just praise, thank you very much. And Susan did offer praise; in fact, she was overgenerous. ("I'm so relieved," she confessed, after reading my work that first time. And one could tell she really was. She had taught in a writing program and knew that having an MFA did not necessarily mean that you could write a sentence.) But because I did not like her fiction—because I saw so little to admire in her use of language, her style—I did not trust what she had to say about writing.

"Other writers try not to use the same word twice in one paragraph. I don't like to use the same word twice on the same *page*." It was a boast—like her much-repeated "I care about every comma." But a more confident writer would not have been so anxiously strict about this, I thought. A more confident writer would not have been as addicted as she was to the thesaurus. Another thing she often depended on while writing was a pal, someone to sit and work with her during the many long hours it took to polish a draft. Sometimes that person would move into the apartment for days at a time, and the two of them would work together in Susan's room, discussing every idea, going over every line, every comma. I have never known any other writer to work like this, though the arrangement obviously helped Susan thrive, and she said she was always much happier when she was working with someone else than when she had to work alone. She hated doing anything alone, and if solitude was a necessity in a writer's life, she would, inasmuch as she could, find ways of getting around it. Also unlike most writers I've known, she liked passing her work around while it was in various stages, showing many drafts to David and to me and to any number of other readers. Once, when I went to pick her up at her house (at a time when David and I were no longer together), as soon as I arrived she handed me a draft of *AIDS and Its Metaphors*. She wanted me to read all one hundred pages of it right then and there; dinner could wait.

On a manuscript page of mine, she circled the word *hurried*. "Think about it. *Do* people actually hurry? Or is that just the way we talk? Don't they really rather hasten? I would change it to 'hastened.'"

I did not take this advice.

In fact, I rejected most of her advice, and this hurt her. It must have seemed arrogant, disrespectful (so it seems to me now; also dumb). And she didn't forget. In later years, she would ask me to give her my work to read, and when I did she would ignore it. Consequently, though she kept asking, I stopped giving her any of my work, and, after a while, she stopped asking. The last time I gave her something (a draft of the opening chapter of what would become my first published book), months passed and still I had not heard from her. At last we had dinner together and I asked her if she'd ever read the chapter. "Of course I read it," she said, bridling as if I had dissed her. "I read it right away." But she would not say one word more.

When I started submitting stories to literary magazines, she behaved as if it were my fault they were rejected. "You need a publication so badly," she said, in a tone that could only demoralize me. And once, in front of several other people, she told me, "Everyone else publishes their crap. Why shouldn't you publish your crap too?"

Many years later, my heart sank when I was told she was in the audience for a reading I was about to give. It was not me she had come to hear (except in passing, we hadn't seen each other in almost a decade) but the two other writers on the program that night, her friends Elizabeth Hardwick and Darryl Pinckney. At the reception after the reading, she said to me only, without any expression, "You read very well."

Not long after that reading, though, I was sitting in my office at Smith College, where I was a visiting professor, when the phone rang. It was Susan. I could not have been more surprised. It seemed she had just learned that I'd received that year's Rome Prize fellowship from the American Academy of Arts and Letters. "You must be so excited," she said. In fact, I almost burst my seams whenever I thought about my year's residency, beginning that fall, at the American Academy in Rome.

"You know, they offered that prize to me once," she said. (I had not known this.) "But I couldn't accept it then. I thought they'd offer it to me again sometime, but they never did." Something about the way she put this made me swallow. I was trying to think what to say when she asked me if I had read *In America*, her fourth, recently published novel. I had not—or, rather, I had read only excerpts from it, in two different literary journals. But I said simply, "Not yet." I started to say something more, but she cut me off. "Look, I didn't call you to chat. I just called to say congratulations." And then she hurried, or *hastened*, off the phone.

She was a natural mentor . . . who hated teaching. Teach as little as possible, she said. Best not to teach at all: "I saw the best writers of my generation destroyed by teaching." She said the life of the writer and the life of the academic would always be at odds. She liked to refer to herself as a self-defrocked academic. She was even prouder to call herself self-created. I never had a mentor, she said. Though she must have learned something from the college professor she married when she was just seventeen. And she'd had other professors, among them Leo Strauss and Kenneth Burke, whom she remembered as extraordinary teachers and for whom she had no end of praise. But however else these men might have inspired her, it was not to be a great teacher herself.

Like many other writers, she equated teaching with failure. (At Columbia, I'd had Richard Yates for one class—

a job to which he showed up each week with his tail between his legs—and I remember him grumbling, "Norman Mailer doesn't have to teach.") Besides, Susan had never wanted to be anyone's employee. The worst part of teaching was that it was, inescapably, a job, and for her to take any job was humiliating. But then, she also found the idea of borrowing a book from the library instead of buying her own copy humiliating. Taking public transportation instead of a cab was deeply humiliating. "When I moved to New York"—at twenty-six, in 1959—"I promised myself, no matter how poor I was, I would never do it." *Stoop* to it, her tone said. Divaism? She seemed to think any self-respecting person would understand and feel as she did.

Going anywhere with her, as soon as you hit the street, she'd stride immediately to the curb, arm raised. In those days, in cold weather, she usually wore a green loden coat. (As I recall, Nicole had a matching one.) The seam had split under one of the arms, and she never got around to having it mended. This was the only time the hole showed: when she was hailing a cab.

I found it strange that there was this one part of her life— the teaching she did, either before or after I met her—that she never talked about. About being a student, she talked a lot. In fact, I'd never known anyone to speak with such reverence about his or her own student days. It gave her a special glow to talk about that time, making me think it must have been the happiest of her life. She said the famously rigorous Hutchins Great Books program at the University of Chicago, where she had earned her bachelor's degree, had made her the mind she was; it was there that she'd learned, if not how to write, how to read closely and how to think critically. She still cherished her course note-books from those days. And she would always take pleasure in buying things like notebooks, pens and pencils, typing paper, and the legal pads that she used for writing long-hand drafts.

Now it occurs to me that at least some of her resistance to teaching might have had to do with her passion for being a student. She had the habits and the aura of a student all her life. She was also, all but physically, always young. People close to her often compared her to a child (her inability to be alone; her undiminishable capacity for wonder; her strong, hero-worshipping side and her need to idolize those she looked up to; her being without health insurance in her forties, when she got cancer, even though health insurance was easily affordable in those days). David and I joked that she was our enfant terrible. (Once, when she was struggling to finish an essay, angry that we weren't being supportive enough, she said, "If you won't do it for me, at least you could do it for Western culture.") My enduring image of her fits exactly that of a student, a fanatical one: staying up all night, surrounded by piles of books and papers, speeding, chain-smoking, reading, taking notes, pounding the typewriter, driven, competitive. She would write that A-plus essay. She would go to the head of the class.

Even her apartment—strictly antibourgeois, unapologetically *ungemütlich*—evoked student life. Its main feature was the growing number of books, but they were mostly paperbacks, and the shelves were cheap pine board. To go with the lack of furniture, there was a lack of decorative objects, there were no curtains or rugs, and the kitchen had only the basics. About six square feet of kitchen space were taken up by an old freezer that hadn't worked in years. A pair of pliers sat on top of the TV set—for changing channels since the knob for that purpose had broken off. People visiting for the first time were clearly surprised to find the celebrated middle-aged writer living like a grad student.

(Everything changes. In her mid-fifties she would say: "I realized I was working just as hard, if not harder, than everyone I knew, and making less money than any of them." And so she transformed that part of her life. But the time I'm talking about was before—before the grand Chelsea penthouse, the enormous library, the rare editions, the art collection, the designer clothes, the country house, the personal assistant, the housekeeper, the personal chef. And one day when I was around the same age she had been when we met, she shook her head at me and said, "What are you planning to do, live like a grad student the rest of your life?")

Whenever some university made her an offer she knew she *shouldn't* refuse, she was torn. Often she turned it down, even though she needed money, and then she would congratulate herself. She was amazed at those who made a much better living from writing than she did yet were still tempted by tenure. She was outraged to hear other writers complain, as many often did, about how their teaching made them miserable because it interfered with their writing. In general, she had contempt for people who didn't do what they truly wanted to do. She believed that most people, unless they were very poor, made their own lives, and, to her, security over freedom was a deplorable choice. It was servile.

She believed that, in our culture, at least, people were much freer than they thought they were and had more options than they seemed willing to acknowledge. She also believed that how other people treated you was, if not wholly, mostly within your control, and she was always after me to *take* that control. "Stop letting people bully you," she would bully me.

She said, "I know you won't believe this, but when I was your age I was a lot more like you than like I am today. And I can prove it!" It turned out that Maria Irene Fornés was coming to visit that day. She and Susan had been a couple between 1959 and 1963. When she arrived, as soon as she'd introduced us, Susan said, "Tell Sigrid what I was like when you met me. Go on, go on!"

"She was an idiot," Fornés said.

When she'd stopped laughing, Susan said to me, "The point I was trying to make is that there's hope for you, too."

"YOU KNOW WHAT would be really fun? Let's all go away somewhere, just for a few days."

She had always loved to travel, a passion David shared, and separately or together, they had already been to many places, both in the States and abroad. Travel was, among other things, an excellent antidote to depression.

It was late autumn, just weeks after her surgery, and Susan, who hated the cold, wanted to go somewhere warm. Fun and warm, and not too far. "You've never been to New Orleans, have you?" No. (This had become a familiar exchange: "You've never seen *The Marriage of Figaro*?" "You've never eaten sushi?" "You've never been to the New York Film Festival?" Each time I said no, Susan would say,

"Ah, you have a treat coming." And it was always so.) She and David had been to New Orleans; they knew people there; it was, they agreed, the perfect destination for a short trip.

We stayed in the French Quarter, though one day some friends took us on a long tour of the bayou. I remember we ate wonderfully ("You've never tasted crawfish?"), and every stranger we met had a story to tell about Mardi Gras. I remember a dinner party where a beautiful young man recited from memory Tennessee Williams's "Mornings on Bourbon Street" and gave me a copy of *In the Winter of Cities*, the book in which that poem appears.

Friends of the beautiful young man invited us to another party, a big fancy party that took place (at a hotel, I believe) the night before we had to fly home. I don't remember where the party was or what it was for, but many of the guests were so extravagantly dressed that it might have been a costume party. At the last minute, we'd gone shopping for something for me to wear. In a vintage clothing store we found a very lovely, very fragile black lace gown. One shoulder strap was broken. But, as my mother used to say, "When you are young, you can get away with anything."

Soon after we arrived at the party, someone introduced us to a large red-faced man dressed in a three-piece white suit, white shirt, white tie, white hat, and white gloves.

"Miz Sontag!" he gasped. "This is a true honor. Why, you look just the same as you do up there on the screen! I've seen every one of your movies. Every single one. Oh, little New Orleans is privileged to have such a great big star in her midst tonight!"

As he kissed my hand, I blushed and started to explain. But Susan, on whom the man had turned his back, had doubled up with laughter and was frantically signaling to me to play along. She had no desire to set the pleasant drunken fellow straight. She was having too much fun.

I have been back to New Orleans just once. It was autumn again, and I stayed in the French Quarter, just as we three had done twenty-eight autumns before. What brought me there the second time was a literary conference. I was on a panel: the topic was "Writers and Masters," and I spoke about Susan as one of my mentors. The next month, she died. It was 2004. How the devastation of the city she loved, just eight months later, would have pierced her.

I never wore that dress again, but I kept it for years— long after I would have been able to get away with wearing it. The book, of course, I still have.

He thought of his friends.
He thought of his lost companion,

. . . .

61

He wept for remembrance.

. . . .

Love. Love. Love.

———————

I DID NOT read most of the obituaries and commentaries that appeared after Susan's death (I have never been much interested in what other people have had to say about her), but I can guess that a number of them mentioned humorlessness, a criticism leveled at her often enough when she was alive. In the index to Craig Seligman's book *Sontag and Kael* (2004), for example, under "Sontag, Susan" we find "humorlessness," followed by eight page references. (Compare this to, say, "Platonism": two page references.) To many, it seems, this deficiency hurt her both as a critic and as an artist. In an article in *The New Yorker*, David Denby writes that her "lack of humor . . . caught up with her" when she started making films, and suggests this was part of the reason that, for all her passion and perceptiveness about filmmaking, her own attempts "turned out terribly." And, if she did have a sense of humor, concludes Phillip Lopate (*Notes on Sontag*, 2009), it "rarely revealed itself on the page."

It is true that reading Susan Sontag doesn't often make you smile. (Surely it's worth noting, however, that her work was selected for *Fierce Pajamas, an Anthology of Humor*

Writing from "The New Yorker," published in 2001.) Also, in public appearances, she often came across as not merely humorless but ill-tempered. Especially during question-and-answer periods, she was inexplicably quick to anger— *I'm surrounded by idiots* was the message her eyes flashed—quick to insult. (The problem, according to her, was the usual one: compared to European audiences, Americans were vulgar and uninformed and their questions were usually trivial.) Still, I've never fully understood why this side of her has drawn so much comment.

Part of the reason undoubtedly has to do with her well-known obsession with seriousness. You must never take yourself too seriously, no matter who you are; there is something comic and even unseemly about those who do—this was a commonplace with which Susan would have nothing to do. She was going to take herself very seriously indeed, whoever might have a problem with that be damned, and the problem *she* had was that others did not always take her seriously enough. Back then, at least, she complained regularly about how some person whose opinion was important to her (always some man, it seemed) had not treated her with proper respect. I myself was astonished at the way she was sometimes dissed. "Miss Sontag, why did you make such a boring movie?" a young man at a screening of *Duet for Cannibals* once asked, and half the audience snickered approvingly. "In twenty-five words or less, could you tell us what the hell that story was about?" Was it because she was a woman that people felt they could address her like this?

Once, at a writers' conference, after Susan had finished speaking, a woman in the audience pushed forward and demanded, "Do you know Jean-Paul Sartre?" "Well," said Susan, "I've met him. I wouldn't say I know him. Why?" The woman's lips twitched with excitement. "Because I heard that you were his mistress." Then, unable to contain herself, she grasped Susan's arm, leaned in, and said, "And *that's* a compliment."

"What was that all about?" was what I wanted to know. "What compliment? Isn't he a decrepit old man now?" The famously unattractive Sartre was in fact seventy-two, twenty-eight years older than Susan (and nearly a foot shorter).

"What it was about," she dryly informed me, "was that a brainy woman *must* have a brainier man."

Of course, being brainy, talented, and very successful doesn't necessarily make you secure. I happened to see her right after she'd finished writing what is probably her most admired short story, "The Way We Live Now."

"I wrote it very fast," she said, "and *for once* I knew right away it was good. Because usually, you know, my first feeling about everything I write is that it's shit."

How much gender had to do with this insecurity is impossible to say. But to think of this proud, intellectually ambitious person coming of age in the days before women's liberation and of the kind of bias she must have routinely encountered, one can imagine how galling it must have been. (A partial list of those who put her down almost as soon as she stepped out of the gate would include Norman Podhoretz, Mary McCarthy, William Buckley, James Dickey, Philip Rahv, John Simon, and Irving Howe.)

She was also insecure in another way. When she worried that she was making too many compromises—agreeing to an interview with *People* magazine, for example, or appearing on television even after denouncing it as "the end of Western civilization"—she would say, "Beckett wouldn't do it." She used to say this all the time. People like Beckett or Kafka or Simone Weil—people whose seriousness she revered—were touchstones for her all her life. Ideally, perhaps, she wanted to be not only serious but "pure," like them.

But, quite naturally, she also wanted to sell books. Make that *had to*, given how she felt about teaching. And it was not just teaching that she resented but almost any gig, such as visiting writer, that she agreed to do for a fee. Very often she turned these visits into disappointing experiences for all. She used to try to get by with little or no preparation, and for her this was not cause for shame. "I don't have a canned lecture," she used to say, implying that having one was not at all something any writer should be proud of. She herself would wing it—with mixed results. Again, as with other public appearances, she was often hostile to her audience, almost as if, weirdly enough, she felt they had no business being there. Certainly she gave the impression that, money aside, she thought she was wasting her time. Somehow, in these situations, even when the audience was made up largely of students, her didactic enthusiasm deserted her. It seemed to be part of her intense dissatisfaction with the world in general. Surely in a just and intelligent society a person who had what she had to contribute would not be expected to perform such drudgery. She should be home, working on the Great Novel that she believed was within her reach. Those who had invited her often ended up as unhappy as she was. She got a reputation for being a monster of arrogance and inconsideration, but, in the way of the world, the invitations kept coming, and she kept accepting them, and her bad reputation grew and grew.

Most people would probably sooner be called homely than humorless, and I doubt Susan was an exception. For one thing, she hated humorlessness in other people; she put the highest value on those who could make her laugh. That was one of the things she liked best about her friend Donald Barthelme. It was one of the things she missed most when her son wasn't there. Surly though she could be, she was never a true curmudgeon. She always had a large circle of friends and acquaintances, and though there was much about her that would have attracted others in any case, is it likely that a truly humorless person—no matter how brilliant, celebrated, or influential—would have had so many people eager to share her company? (Also, I could be wrong, but I believe a woman is more likely than a man is to be damned for a deficiency of humor; a humorless man doesn't seem to have quite the same off-putting aspect as a humorless woman. And we shouldn't forget, either, that feminists are by definition humorless, aren't they? Remember "How many feminists does it take to change a lightbulb?")

She laughed easily—and she was not a snob about humor, either; she appreciated even feeble attempts. She laughed when someone told her what was supposedly Freud's favorite joke: "Have you taken a bath?" "No, why? Is one missing?" She laughed at the awful pun someone else made on a name well known in translating—"Hong if you like Kierkegaard"—and at my imitation of Woody Woodpecker. In keeping with her passion for sharing whatever pleased her, she was eager to repeat any amusing thing she might have heard. But she bemoaned the fact that she was no good at telling jokes, or stories for that matter. If she knew a funny story that David also knew, she'd insist he be the one to tell it because "he tells it funnier than I do." About his undeniably superb comic flair, she said, "He didn't get that from me."

"I know only one joke," she said. "And I tell it very badly. It's a Jewish joke, of course." And she tried to tell it with a Yiddish accent. A mother. A neurotic child. "Doctor, Doctor, vot should I do? Every time my little boy sees kreplach, he starts to scream." The punch line required that Susan, as the mother, clutch her head between her hands and, with an expression of stark fear, scream, "*Aaahh! Kreplaaaaach!*" This remains one of the funniest things I've ever seen.

Another memory. She walks into the kitchen, sits down at the kitchen counter with me, and says, "I just got a very interesting phone call. It was some guy who said he was doing a survey for the Maidenform company, and would I take a minute to answer a couple of questions. So I said sure. And then he started asking things like, was I wearing a bra right now, what kind of bra was it, and what size was it—"

"You mean an obscene phone call."

She looks puzzled, then sheepish. "That would explain it."

Final note: after her hair, the feature of hers that struck people most was her big, beautiful smile.

———

WHEN, RECENTLY, I learned that Javier Marías said that the worst thing a writer can do is to take himself or his work too seriously, I think I understood. I think I even agree with him. I think if I had thought this way myself when I was young, my life could have been happier. I might even have turned out to be a better writer. Nevertheless, I am grateful to have had as an early model someone who held such an exalted, unironic view of the writer's vocation. ("And you must *think* of it as a vocation. Never as a career.")

Virginia Woolf lived as if literature were a religion and she one of its priests. Susan made me think of the anti-quated hyperbole of Thomas Carlyle: the writer as hero. There could *be* no nobler pursuit, no greater adventure, no more rewarding quest. And she shared Woolf's worship of books, her idea of heaven as eternal reading. (Though she surely would have opposed Woolf's idea that there was such a thing in literature as "a woman's sentence"; she would not even allow that there was such a thing in the world as a woman's point of view.)

She said, "Pay no attention to these writers who claim you can't be a serious writer and a voracious reader at the same time." (Two such writers, I recall, were V. S. Naipaul and Norman Mailer.) After all, what mattered was the life of the mind, and for that life to be lived fully, reading was *the* necessity. Aiming for a book a day was not too high (though it was something I myself could not achieve). Be-cause of her, I began reading too fast.

Because of her, I began writing my name in each new book I acquired. I began clipping articles from newspapers and magazines and filing them in various books. Like her, I always read with a pencil in hand (never a pen), for underlining.

From Professor Hardwick, though she was at times encouraging, I always got the feeling that if I gave myself over completely to the writer's life I would find more unhappiness than fulfillment. For years after I'd studied with her, whenever we spoke I noticed she almost always asked about my writing only after she'd asked about my love life: "Do you still have that nice young man?" (Long after it was true, I kept answering yes just to avoid hearing her groan, "Don't tell me you've lost another one.") Once, after not seeing her for several years, I told her I was thinking of having a child, and I was deeply moved by her response: "Now, that's *one* decision you'll *never* regret." Deeply moved but also deeply anxious, because of what seemed to lie beneath that remark. (I never had the child, and I confess that, when I read how, toward the end of her life, Woolf decided that, books or no books, fame or no fame, not having children meant that her life must finally be judged a failure, I felt betrayed.) Hardwick used to tell her Barnard students that you had to be really bored with life to become a writer. Somehow I don't believe she thought this was true for men.

With Susan, on the other hand, I felt as if I were being given permission to devote myself to these two vocations—

reading and writing—that were so often difficult to justify. And it was clear that, no matter how hard or frustrating or daunting it was—and no matter how much like a long punishment writing a book could be—she would not have chosen any other way; she would not have wanted any other life than the life she had.

"A writer's standards can't ever possibly be too high."

"Never worry about being obsessive. I like obsessive people. Obsessive people make great art."

She liked outsiders, too. It pleased her to see herself as an outsider.

And just because you were born an American didn't mean you couldn't cultivate a European mind.

To read a whole shelf of books to research one twenty-page essay, to spend months writing and rewriting, going through one entire ream of typing paper before those twenty pages could be called done—for the serious writer, this was, of course, normal. And, of course, you didn't do it to feel good about yourself. ("My first feeling about everything I write is that it's shit.") You didn't do it for your own enjoyment (unlike reading), or for catharsis, or to express yourself, or to please some particular audience. You did it for literature, she said. And there was nothing wrong with never being satisfied with what you did. (Indeed, if you weren't regularly tormented by self-doubt, your work probably *was* shit.)

71

"The question you have to ask yourself is whether what you're writing is necessary." I didn't know about this. *Necessary?* That way, I thought, lies writer's block.

Because of her, I would resist switching from typewriter to word processor. "You want to *slow down,* not speed up. The last thing you want is something that's going to make writing *easier.*" She was loath as well to make the change from record albums to CDs. She was skeptical of new gadgets and electronic devices. Being low-tech was a source of pride to her.

But one way in which she considered herself a terrible model was in her work habits. She had no discipline, she said. She could not steel herself to write every day, as everyone knew was best. But it was not so much lack of discipline (or the laziness she sometimes reproached herself for) as her hunger to do many other things besides write. She wanted to travel a lot and go out every night—and to me, the most fitting of all the things that were said upon her death was by Hardwick: "In the end, nothing is more touching to the emotions than to think of her own loss of evenings at 'happenings,' at dance recitals, the opera, movies."

Lincoln Center. For the rest of my life, I think, I will never hear the orchestra tuning up or watch the chandeliers rise toward the ceiling of the opera house without remembering her.

To get herself to work, she had to clear out big chunks of time during which she would do nothing else. She would take Dexedrine and work around the clock, never leaving the apartment, rarely leaving her desk. We'd go to sleep to the sound of her typing and wake up to the sound of her typing. And though she often said she wished she could work in a less self-destructive way, she believed it was only after going at it full throttle for many hours that your mind really started to click and you'd come up with your best ideas.

She used to say that if she hadn't been a writer she would have been a doctor. Certainly, she possessed the necessary stamina. But I think the particular kind of discipline and submission to routine required of any physician would have been beyond her.

She said a writer should never pay attention to reviews, good or bad. "In fact, you'll see, the good ones will often make you feel even worse than the bad ones." Besides, she said, people are sheep. If one person says something's good, the next person says it's good, and so on. "And if *I* say something's good, *everyone* says it's good." At a certain point, people didn't even *look* at the work anymore; they simply made up their minds about it based on what had already been said about it.

But there were times when she was piqued about the

person to whom one of her books had been assigned for review because she didn't believe that person was smart enough or important enough to write about her.

She said it was a mistake to care too much if others liked or disliked you. To be despised in certain circumstances, or by certain people, could be a high compliment.

She said, "Don't be afraid to steal. I steal from other writers all the time." And she could point to no few instances of writers stealing from her.

She said, "Beware of ghettoization. Resist the pressure to think of yourself as a woman writer." (I winced when I entered a bookstore recently and saw her shelved under the sign Celebrate Women's History Month. Just her, Anaïs Nin, and Zora Neale Hurston.)

She said, "Resist the temptation to think of yourself as a victim." (She had no patience with weaklings who couldn't take care of themselves; those without armor brought out her aggression.) She believed that women were raised to be masochists and that this, too, was something a woman had to struggle against. Though she saw herself as utterly different from most other women, she deplored what she saw as her own masochistic tendencies. "Like my grotesque way of panting after people who don't want me." (*Grotesque* was another one of her words.)

———————

I HAD HEARD before I ever saw it that Susan's apartment was a well-known crash pad. (She confirmed a story about the arrival on her doorstep of Jean Genet, whose first words were "Do you have any eggs?", and told me another: "He was totally paranoid about being recognized. He was afraid the police were after him because of his association with the Black Panthers. I kept telling him no one would recognize him here, and then the very first time we leave the building a man across the street walks over and says, 'Aren't you Jean Genet?'") I was aware that some of Susan's New York friends, unsure what to do with some acquaintance visiting from out of town, would sometimes send that person, especially if it was a young person, uptown to her. While I lived at 340 there was often someone sleeping on the single bed that had been moved from the former maid's room (now my study) into a corner of the living room.

At that time, partly because of her highly regarded and popular essays on photography, and partly because of her outspokenness about having cancer, Susan was riding a second wave of celebrity (the first, of course, having crested in the sixties, with the appearance of her first critical essays, most famously "Notes on 'Camp'"). The phone rang all day long, and Susan had no desire to get an answering machine or service. Living with someone as hyperactive as

Susan was already like living with a crowd, but there was also a steady stream of visitors. Susan loved to go out, but she also loved to have people, including those she was meeting for the first time, come to her. Home was where she gave most of her interviews, for example. It seemed to me I was forever opening the door to some stranger, or coming home to find someone waiting for her (sometimes for up to an hour) in the kitchen, where, though it was the smallest room in the house, she tended to receive guests. She also liked to have people she was going out with pick her up at home, even if wherever they were going was in a whole other part of town.

David, of course, was used to his mother's busy, people-filled life. As she liked to say, he had grown up "on coats," meaning she had dragged him along to the many parties and "happenings" and other events she had not wanted to miss just because she had a young child. (She would also take him to the movies and let him sleep in his seat while she watched a double feature.) In fact, though he had a much stronger sense of privacy than Susan did, like her, he grew bored and restless when things were too quiet. He also had her stamina, and though he was perhaps some-what less social than she, he was far more social than I, who already carried the seeds of the person I would become: someone who spends ninety percent of her time alone.

I have never been the kind of person who wants to do

many things; I have always wanted to do only one thing well. The opposite of Susan, who could not help seeing my way as a failing, even if it was also the way of many artists, including most dancers, a type of artist she adored. (She'd probably heard the story about Balanchine, whom someone once tried unsuccessfully to take to a museum. "I've been to a museum," Mr. B is supposed to have said.) Both she and David disapproved of the monkish streak in me; in their eyes, it showed a certain lack of vitality and curiosity—very bad in a would-be writer! To David, it suggested a kind of weakness, a weakness that, if indulged, would make me boring. Susan believed that the reclusive type was, at heart, cold and selfish. I should change.

And I did try to change. For a time, I tried very hard to keep up. After all, it wasn't that I didn't enjoy going out, too. And of course I was excited to meet the many brilliant writers and artists Susan knew. (Susan: "When I was a kid in school, I remember how people would point to a certain desk and say, 'That's where Cyd Charisse sat!' And I was thrilled, too. And now, my God, when I think how much I take for granted.") Some of the nicest times I recall were visits to the country house of Roger and Dorothea Straus, who were very kind. (On hearing that Susan and David had bought themselves tennis rackets—they were about to take lessons from a pro who happened also to be one of our neighbors—Roger left the room and returned carrying one of his own rackets. "For you, dear." I never once used it, but, like the black lace dress, I held on to it for many years.)

Of course I wanted to go to Studio 54. ("You've never met Andy Warhol?")

But when you're in love, what is it that you want more than anything else in the world? Looking back, I can hardly remember times when David and I were alone. Once or twice I went and stayed with him for a night in the room he rented (though rarely used) in Princeton, and I remember wishing dolefully that we could be there all the time.

Soon after I moved into 340, I started working again at *The New York Review*. After putting in my hours as one of Robert Silvers's three assistants (and given Susan's connection as a contributor to the *Review*, her friendship with the editors, and her fanatical interest in everything that went on there, the line between my work life and my home life was pretty blurred), often the last thing I wanted to do was go out—especially somewhere noisy and glitzy and crowded. (When I got sick of being faulted for not being more like the two of them, for not getting out in the world more, for not wanting to see and do more, I'd retaliate with what was probably the biggest gun I had: "Beckett wouldn't do it.")

Susan used to say how much easier it was for her to work in her room if she knew there were other people elsewhere in the apartment. But the only time I could work seemed to be when the apartment was empty.

For a while, I tried getting up very early and locking myself in my study. But as soon as Susan was awake, she would knock and ask me to join her in the kitchen. (She slept as little as possible; you could not convince her that there was any value in the activity of the unconscious mind; sleep, like childhood, was a waste of time.) She couldn't bear to have her morning coffee or read the newspaper alone. In fact, fresh out of bed she seemed especially in need of an ear. She would talk nonstop about whatever came into her head, and for some reason at that hour she was often roiling with indignation. Something about her life that was bothering her, or maybe something she saw on the front page of the *Times*, would set her off. At such moments she reminded me to a remarkable degree of my German mother—another touchy, chronic ranter who thought she was surrounded by idiots, who practically lived in a state of indignation, and who happened also to share Susan's contempt for American superficiality and American "culture."

David found this morning Susan difficult. He'd sit at the kitchen counter with his back turned, deep in the paper, face curtained by his long dark hair.

She simply could not bear to be alone. Among the many things she always wanted to do, there was none that she would have chosen to do all by herself. There was no experience, as far as she was concerned, that could be enhanced by being undertaken solo. For her, having to do certain things, such as eat a meal, without company was like a punishment. She would rather have gone out to dinner with someone she didn't even much care for than eat in alone.

"You will notice," she once told me, "that I'm always doing something. If I weren't talking to you right now, I'd be reading." She always made sure her mind was occupied. In the absence of distraction, she said, her mind went blank, and she compared it to the static on the screen when a TV channel stops broadcasting. She told me this, I know she did. I remember her words. I have thought of them very often since, but I still have trouble believing them. A blank screen . . . and nothing to project? No daydreams, no fantasies, no musings or memories, no thoughts about works in progress, about life, about people, about things she was planning to do—no *thoughts* at all? How was that possible?

No, I did not understand. But it certainly helped explain her outsize needs: manic activity, constant company. It helped explain her dislike of the country, and why it was so much harder for her than for most people to call it a day. That blank screen, she made clear, was a thing greatly to be feared. It might also explain why, despite her curiosity, despite her hunger for new, even risky experience ("I intend to do everything," she told her diary when she was sixteen), and despite her immersion in the counterculture, she steered clear of mind-altering drugs. (There was a certain kind of person who was generally thought of as a bad candidate for LSD, the kind of person you didn't ever want to be caught tripping with. She was that person.)

I thought of that blank screen again when I read David's description of Susan's final bout with cancer, when the thought of extinction caused her such anguish and terror she was driven almost insane.

It wasn't enough that she had spent the evening out with friends. When she came home, though it was late, though David and I might be already in bed, she would knock. "May I come in?" Well, we were expecting her. (The shyness in her voice through that closed door was heartbreaking.) David and I slept on a mattress on the floor. A small sofa stood near it. She would settle on the sofa, light a cigarette, and begin telling us all about her evening. I sometimes fell asleep while she was still talking.

The stage IV breast cancer, the breakup with Nicole—up till then, there had probably never been a time in her life when she feared being alone as much as she did now. She made no attempt to hide how devastating it would be for her if David were to move out. It was impossible even to think about what I wanted without feeling selfish and cruel. "I don't think I could survive the guilt," David said, in the last conversation he and I would have on the subject.

Unsurprisingly, she was defensive. She insisted that it was not primarily neediness but rather love that made her want to keep her son with her forever. Theirs had never been an ordinary mother-son relationship, she said. In fact, she told me, she had never really wanted David to think of her as his mother. "I'd rather he see me as—oh, I don't know—his goofy big sister." ("More like my brother" and "my best friend" was how she said *she* usually thought of *him*.) After all, she had been just nineteen when he was born. (This always bewildered me: the emphasis on their "closeness" in age, as if many other women back then hadn't had babies at around the same age—my own mother, for example, who'd been even younger; as if Susan and David were anywhere near the same generation.) And she had made him. They were so alike as to be almost identical in some ways, sharing most of the same tastes and the same interests and the same passions.

She showed me a photograph that she cherished, the young Roland Barthes with his mother: already quite a big boy at the time and thus a little comical to behold, aloft in the arms of *maman*, long legs dangling. Roland Barthes, one of Susan's greatest literary heroes, greatly admired by me as well, had lived with his mother till the day she died.

There was nothing wrong with the three of us sharing a roof. Indeed, in other cultures—for example, in Russia ("Isn't that right, Joseph?")—an arrangement like ours would have been common.

And tell her, please, what was so terrific about the traditional nuclear family? Hadn't she publicly pronounced it "a disaster"? (She also frequently railed against couples: no matter how interesting one or both people might be when you saw them separately, when you saw them together they were invariably boring.)

Don't be so conventional. (The truth was, I had grown up in a very unconventional household, and ordinary bourgeois existence was, I confess, not only attractive but frankly exotic to me.)

What did it matter what other people said?

She was right: I should not have cared what other people said. But I did care. And what they said was shocking. People felt free to say things to me they would never have dared say to her.

That there was feverish, prurient interest swirling around 340 was something I already knew. Before I ever met Susan or David, I'd heard the talk. Now people came straight out and asked: *Is it true? Have they had sex together?* Sometimes, rather than being asked, I was told: *They must have had sex together.* My presence in the household seemed to intensify speculation, bringing the pot to a boil. (The fact of

Susan's bisexuality was, of course, highly pertinent.) *What was going on up there?* One night, after I had moved out, but before David and I broke up, we had dinner with an NYU professor with whom David was just then becoming friends. At one point, this man turned to him and said, "Did you and Sigrid and Susan sleep together?" When David said, "*What?*" he simply repeated the question more slowly, as if to a foreigner or an idiot.

And what about all the other talk about Susan? Was it true? Was she really a monster like everyone said? I was always amazed at how badly people spoke of Susan and never able to tell how aware of this she was herself. (If she had any idea how widespread—and accepted—the rumors that she had behaved immorally with her son were, she never spoke of it to me.) In 1982, after a Manhattan Town Hall rally in support of Poland's Solidarity movement, at which she denounced Communism as essentially a variant of fascism, she was stunned by the violence with which she was attacked. "I never knew I had so many enemies." But to me, it sometimes seemed she had more enemies than anyone else I'd ever met. And, as happens in powerful circles, even some of her friends were her enemies.

I don't know if it was true what she'd been told, that a certain editor at *The New Yorker* had vowed Susan Sontag would never publish a story in that magazine so long as he worked there, but it sounds plausible; it was the kind of feeling she provoked. (When, in 1977, *The New Yorker* published her story "Unguided Tours," she was as giddily triumphant as if it were the first thing she'd ever published in her life.)

I don't know, either, if she was right when she attributed the nasty response to her Town Hall appearance mostly to envy. I do know that envy—serious, seething, spiteful envy—stalked her everywhere she went. (But the Town Hall rally was one occasion where she regretted not being better prepared; if she'd spent more time on her remarks, she might have found a way to express them that would not have been so inciting.)

What was going on up there?

I remember one friend who laughed and said, "Everyone imagines the most outrageous scenarios when in fact what you've got is your classic possessive, controlling mother and guilt-ridden son."

I found it difficult that Susan wanted to talk so much about her and David's history, and that that history was filled with so much conflict and resentment. She would tick off all the things she had done for David, her face flushed, her voice rising. Had *she* had a mother like that? Had *I* had a mother like that? Comparing herself with other parents she knew, she often mistook their willingness to grant their children a large measure of independence for a lack of caring. (She was often critical of the way other people treated their children, and in fact I am unable to recall her ever speaking highly of anyone as a parent.)

But, for all her pride in her motherhood, and for all her laments about not having had more kids, she was not maternal. In fact, I found it almost impossible to imagine her nursing, or tending to an infant or a small child. I could more easily imagine her digging ditches or break-dancing or milking a cow. From the time she knew she was pregnant until the day she went into labor, she never saw a doctor. "I didn't know you were supposed to."

Endlessly curious, at least one book a day, but not one book about pregnancy or child care. She liked to tell a story about the time a group of other young mothers approached her to express concern about her parenting, suggesting she needed guidance. It wasn't that they were busybodies, she said. They were just unliberated fifties women stuck with conventional ideas of what a proper woman, wife, and mother should be. I asked her if they had made her feel guilty, and she replied emphatically *no*. She had never felt any guilt about the kind of mother she was. "Not one iota."

And she told this story: "Everyone warned me that after David was born I wouldn't get much sleep. But they were wrong. He never woke me up. From the day I brought him home from the hospital, he always slept straight through the night." Clearly, this was how she remembered it. Clearly, she had no idea it could not be true.

And this: "When I was writing the last pages of *The Benefactor*, I didn't eat or sleep or change clothes for days. At the very end, I couldn't even stop to light my own cigarettes. I had David stand by and light them for me while I kept typing." When she was writing the last pages of *The Benefactor*, it was 1962, and David was ten.

She was not a mom. Every once in a while, noticing how dirty David's glasses were, she'd pluck them from his face and wash them at the kitchen sink. I remember thinking how it was the only momish thing I ever saw her do. And I noticed that when she was around children—for example, the Strauses' three little granddaughters—she paid no attention to them.

People who'd known Susan for years, who'd watched David grow up, said they didn't believe she would ever let him go. It had nothing to do with cancer, they said; she would never let another person come first in her son's life. She herself said that, because of the intense, complicated nature of their relationship, "David and I have always needed to have a third person around." She didn't like the word *girl-friend* much; she preferred *friend*, though she sometimes referred to me jovially as David's *consort*. She referred to the three of us as the duke and duchess and duckling of Riverside Drive. I knew that wasn't good. It didn't help, either, that whatever fun thing David wanted to do she wanted to do with him—tennis lessons, *motorcycle* lessons. And although she kept telling me she would be happy to support not just David and me but any child of ours as well, she also said that for David to become a father anytime soon would ruin his life.

"Why don't you two just do sixty-nine? Then you won't have to worry about birth control." There was a fourth person at the lunch table the day Susan said this, and it was he who broke the silence. "Looks like Susan doesn't want to be a grandmother."

It was a time of great discomfort and confusion and constraint for me—a time when I cut myself off from other people, including family and friends. Though I had little privacy or solitude, I felt isolated in a way I never had before. I learned to be wary of those who hoped to use me to get closer to Susan. ("Oh, and please bring your mother" was something David had grown accustomed to hearing when he was coming of age and invited various places.) And it was hard, in the midst of all that literary celebrity, both at home and at work—it was hard, trying to find one's own way. And it could be mortifying, trying to stand up for one's own unpublished, amateur pages, kicking up a fuss about the importance of one's time. When I tried to talk to Susan about how she shouldn't interrupt me while I was trying to write, or be constantly asking me to do things for her, such as ordering long lists of books for her own library while I was at the office, she would promise to change. And she might change, briefly, but then she almost immediately fell back into her old ways.

———

SHE TRIED TO talk me out of going to the writers' colony. It would be bad for my relationship with David, she said. He and I had been together less than a year; it was too soon for us to be separated for a whole month. But I knew that my going would have to bring David at least some relief; we had been fighting a lot, and he was getting sick of seeing me cry. (More advice from Susan: If you cry once, people feel sorry for you. But if you cry every day, they just think you're a drag.) She was worried also that, if I went away, I might meet someone else. She thought I was a hopeless flirt. She also called me a cocktease—not so much in disapproval as in the spirit of sharing: "I've always been called that myself."

She felt vindicated when things didn't work out for me. Hadn't she tried to tell me that running off to the middle of nowhere was not going to help me write? Though I wrote every day, I got only a pitifully small amount done, none of it good. I ended up throwing those pages away.

When I got back to the city, it was the beginning of spring. Early that summer, Leonard Michaels, who taught at Berkeley, was directing a writers' conference. He had invited Susan to be on the faculty. Though glad for any excuse for a trip to California, as always she did not want to go alone. She might easily have gone with one of her friends, Elizabeth Hardwick or Donald Barthelme or Theodore Solotaroff, all of whom had also been invited to the weeklong conference. But she wanted to take David along—and why not his consort ("You've never been to California?") as well. The nice folks at Berkeley agreed to arrange for an extra room. Then we decided to turn it into a vacation by staying on for another week once Susan's duties at the conference were done.

I wanted to go. I had never been to the West Coast before. I was excited about seeing Berkeley and San Francisco for the first time, and it was my idea to rent a car and drive down to Big Sur for a couple of days as well. This part of the trip was not something Susan would have planned; she'd already been to Big Sur, for one thing, and she was not interested in natural scenery, no matter how sublime—not when she could sit hour upon hour at the Pacific Film Archive instead while movie after movie was screened for her. It was the perfect chance for David and me to go off and do something alone together; it was the part of the trip I was looking forward to most.

But when the day came, Susan decided she was going to Big Sur, too. It was not so much that she wanted to see Big Sur again as that she could not bear to be left behind. Not that she would have been alone; from the day we arrived she'd been surrounded by people, including various friends of hers who lived in the Bay Area, all of them eager to hang out with her. Indeed, she'd made a date for the following day with one of them, who'd promised to take her to the best restaurant in Chinatown for lunch. Which meant that our trip had to be cut short. "But so what? It's not the destination that matters," she said, "it's the drive, isn't it?" I am not proud of the way I behaved on that drive. What made her coming along even more maddening and painful for me was that, at the end of the week, I would be flying back home by myself while the two of them would go on together to visit Susan's parents in Hawaii.

She took a deep breath before she spoke. "David tells me you're thinking of moving out and that it's because of me." We were where it all began: in her room, I sitting on her desk chair, she on her bed. "I'm sorry," she said, modulating her voice and hitting her consonants as she did when she wished to sound in control, "but I cannot take that responsibility."

There really wasn't much I could say to that.

"It's not fair," she said stubbornly. "What if he doesn't forgive me for your moving out?"

She said, "My dear, you haven't thought this through. You don't go from being a couple that lives together to a couple that lives apart. That's absurd. You're making a huge mistake."

I'd have only myself to blame if we broke up.

If only it hadn't been impossible for her to be alone. If only her relationship with Nicole could have been saved. If only she'd still been living half the time on rue de la Faisanderie. If only Joseph had wanted to be her man. If only she hadn't gotten cancer.

We would have broken up anyway. We would have lasted longer, definitely. But in the end, things would not have worked out. Susan could have lived on the moon, and David and I would not have worked out. I've known this for a long time. What I don't know is how we managed to stagger on for another year and a half after I moved out.

For several months, we continued to spend most of our time together at 340 rather than in the half-furnished shoe box with unreliable heat and hot water that I had rented on Sullivan Street. During that time, things actually did improve—meaning, we got along better. I wasn't happy, but I was more at peace. I was no longer working at *The New York Review* but at a similar job, as assistant to the editor of a small German publishing house in a funky loft in newly named Tribeca. And I had started writing a novel. It would be published only as excerpts in a small magazine, it would be scorned by Hardwick as "bad, every word of it, not worth writing," but when it was only a few chapters long it got me a literary agent and the attention of a couple of editors.

It just hit me. That Berkeley conference. Susan. Hardwick. Leonard Michaels. Donald Barthelme. Theodore Solotaroff. They're all dead. Most of the people in this memoir are dead.

Right after I moved, someone sent me an anonymous letter beginning with "Congratulations" and going on to say that I had done a brave, smart, probably lifesaving thing. It was meant to be supportive, of course. But I knew exactly why it was anonymous, and all it did was infuriate me. (I felt much the same way when, years later, a friend of Susan's reminisced: "Of course, from the day you moved in with them, we all just looked on in *horror*.")

· · · ·

The year 1978 brought something Susan had long been dreading: the expiration of her lease. Being forced to leave her home of nearly ten years threw her into a crisis. She even had bad dreams about it, including one in which she found herself expected to live in a house that had no roof over it. "But what about when it rains?" she kept asking the dream landlord. (Eerily, a fire in an apartment she would rent some years later in a town house on King Street would destroy part of her roof.) She would not really be satisfied with either of the next two apartments she lived in, though both were such nice apartments I could not see why. She would not be truly happy again until she found herself in another penthouse, this one in Chelsea, where, as on Riverside Drive, she had splendid views of the Hudson.

Her last home.

The months spent searching for a new apartment were a troubled time for David and Susan, who were sometimes not even on speaking terms. It became increasingly troubled for David and me as well, not least because I had started seeing someone else. ("I understand why you did it, but why on earth did you have to tell him?" was Susan's exasperated take on this. So much she did not understand.) In fact, 1978 stands out in my memory as one of the bleakest and most discouraging years of my life. Susan finally signed a lease on a duplex on East 17th Street. I was there on the unseasonably hot spring day they moved in, but not very often after that. I can't recall ever spending a night there, though I know I did. David and I began seeing less of each other, and sometime during the following winter we had one last fight.

When I was packing to move out of 340, Susan told me I could take anything I wanted. I took two toys I had found in the depths of David's closet: a Raggedy Andy doll and a small brown bear with one eye missing. (Years later, Susan would laugh off an interviewer's comment regarding David's complaints about his unhappy childhood, saying she remembered his room being full of toys, and claiming: "I still have his teddy bear.")

———————

IN THE YEARS after David and I broke up, I had more contact with Susan than I had with him, though it never amounted to much. During this time she was often depressed. Against her advice, David had accepted the job that Roger Straus had offered him upon his graduation from Princeton. (In Susan's eyes, working as an editor was beneath David; she believed great books were within his reach, too, and that he should allow her to keep supporting him while he devoted himself to writing.) Then, to her dismay, he finally moved into a place of his own. Always when I saw her now she complained of being lonely, of feeling rejected, abandoned. Sometimes she wept. She had gotten it into her head that everything she ever did in her life was first of all to win David's love and respect. As if he were the parent and she the child.

She talked about being in therapy—a huge surprise, for I remembered how much disdain she once had for people who resorted to therapy, or, worse, took antidepressants. Among people she knew, the ones she seemed to respect most were the ones who, no matter how unhappy they were, had resisted therapy. The exemplary response to depression was stoicism, and for all she might countenance the saturnine temperament in a genius like Walter Benjamin (a temperament she believed she shared), she had little patience with an ordinary person's moods. Unless you had what she called a real problem—life-threatening illness, for example—if you were depressed, you'd do better to try to hide it from her. For the suicidal, she had not much empathy. I was startled when she told me that, any time the thought of suicide ever occurred to her, she heard a voice inside her say, "They're not going to get *me*." (Who's "they"? I wondered.)

But, in her early fifties, her own chronic irritability and discontent shaded into something darker. She found herself crawling back into bed soon after getting up, and her memory and concentration were at times so poor that, she said, "I really thought I might have had a mini-stroke." She consulted a neurologist who set her straight: no stroke, just your typical midlife clinical depression. She'd started seeing a psychiatrist; for a while she'd even taken Elavil. And now, psychotherapy had become one of her enthusiasms. She talked at length about her sessions, sharing what she'd told the therapist and what the therapist had told her—including, among other things, that one of Susan's problems was that she was surrounded by narcissists whom she didn't understand because she was not a narcissist herself. ("What about you?" she asked me earnestly. "Are you a narcissist?")

"Why did you try to make a father out of your son?"

At first when she heard this, Susan said, she was shocked. She didn't know *where* the therapist could have come up with *that*! But then it hit her, she said: she *had* tried to do that. And we both started to cry.

I remember, on the way home from New Orleans, the two of us waiting while David went to take care of our luggage. The airport was very crowded. He was gone a long time, we both grew a little anxious, but at last we saw him, still a ways off but easy to spot because of his height. And Susan spoke of what a comfort this always was to her: being somewhere, waiting for him, and finally catching sight of him, "this giraffe loping toward you."

Besides tallness, he had two other features she found attractive in both men and women: a deep voice and a large head.

She called herself a melancholic, but that is too wan and passive a word for what afflicted her. She was not what the French mean by *un triste*. Her sadness was full of darkest rage. She reacted by kicking and screaming. They weren't going to get *her*! When she was unhappy with the world, she lashed out; she wanted to hurt someone. In her inner circle she always had at least one whipping boy, or girl, and she would strike and strike and strike.

Except for those she considered important, or who intimidated her, she often browbeat or criticized her friends. She defended her behavior by saying she believed in "calling people on things," or "correcting" them, as if it was a question of Truth. People needed to be *told*. But she told them unkindly, and often when there were others present. In fact, it was when there was an audience that she was likely to really go to town. At the worst of such times, I'd flash on the image of her as a girl drinking those glasses of blood. A few people figured out that if you stood up to her, if you bared your own teeth and snarled in return, she'd back down.

But she also took out her temper on strangers. That time

we went to Philadelphia, she got into a fight with the hotel desk clerk. He grew flustered and made a slip: "Mr. Sontag—"

"I am not Mr. Sontag," she rapped out. "And if you would just pick up your head and look at me you would see that."

David explained that, although this kind of behavior was not entirely new, it had become much worse since the cancer, to the point where it seemed she could not resist such confrontations. But if these confrontations gave her release, they could also make being in public with her difficult. It would have been different if she'd reserved her tongue-lashings for people who'd actually done something unforgivable, but this was not the case. All a clerk or a waiter had to do was be less than alacritous to serve her, or make a careless mistake, and she'd respond as if deeply affronted. Her goal then was not just to express her displeasure but to humiliate that person. "I know you probably think you're much too good for this job . . ." she'd begin.

She was a masochist *and* a sadist.

When her therapist suggested that Susan must have been "so angry" when she got cancer, and angry again when her home was damaged by an accidental fire, Susan's response was genuine puzzlement. "I said, but wouldn't that be irrational? Like, I'm supposed to be angry at— what? A state of affairs?" But the anger aroused in her by ordinary service people was just as irrational. There was too much loathing in it. And there were times when I couldn't help wondering, How is it possible to feel that much loathing for someone you don't even know? Sometimes she'd request something special—a substitution for a dish on the menu, for example—and when told she couldn't have it she'd say, "Don't get excited! I was just asking." She was forever telling people not to get excited, in a tone mordant with contempt.

In restaurants, I found her behavior downright foolhardy. Had she never heard of waiter's revenge?

At a coffee shop in SoHo that she began frequenting while living on King Street, she was finally asked not to come back.

She often mentioned how much she loved to apologize. "I always feel *wonderful* after." But I never heard her apologize or express any regret for one of her outbursts. She seemed to think it was her right to tell people off, and that quickness to anger was not a besetting weakness but one of her strengths.

She was outraged to be thought of as a monster, but, when speaking of rivals, she enjoyed quoting a saying that had been popular when she was growing up: "It's like putting a baby in the ring with Joe Louis." (She was Joe Louis.)

But I used to think that a man who behaved as she did would probably have learned long ago, at the hands of other men, a thing or two about respect.

. . .

In spite of all her passions, her huge appetite for beauty and pleasure, her famous avidity, and the unflagging pace of her enviably rich life, she was mortally malcontented, and hers was a restlessness no amount of travel was going to cure. And in spite of her undeniable achievements, all the hard-won honors and well-deserved acclaim, a sense of failure clung to her like widow's weeds. Early on, this had everything to do with how her fiction had been received. It would always vex her, the way people acted as if she had come to fiction writing as some kind of afterthought, when, *hello*, her first book had been a novel. That book had been snatched up by a first-rate publisher before it was even finished; she'd had every reason to think that, as a novelist, she was on her way. Thanks to a supreme gift for essay writing, things would go well, *wildly* so; but that success was not the answer to her dreams.

By the time I met Susan, her two novels had been so forgotten that even many of her fans did not know they existed. I myself had assumed *Against Interpretation* was her first book (a widespread and abiding misbelief, repeated most recently by her own publisher in the author bios of the two books that have appeared since her death).

Two and a half decades would pass before she was able to finish another novel (though she began several), but she never stopped writing short stories. Though most of her stories would be published, it was hard not to suspect that some had been accepted more because of her name than because of their merits. For, when a story appeared, the response was nothing like the warm praise she was used to receiving when she brought out an essay. (And when she turned to filmmaking, the response would be even colder.)

It wounded her that the fiction writers whose work she admired and championed did not admire her work in return. In fact, there seemed to be no strong champions of her fiction, not even among her friends. She got used to hearing that she'd do better to stick to what she did so brilliantly (in some eyes, perhaps better than anyone else). This put her (or, more accurately, she put herself) in the position of being her own champion. She was forever defending her fiction, trying to win it attention, pushing it on people who did not appreciate it. An awkward and demoralizing position. In private and in public, again and again, she insisted that, regardless of what everyone else might say, she was a fiction writer who happened to write essays and not the other way around. That no one bought this was one of the biggest frustrations of her life. But she did not give up. Again, she believed that a large part of how other people treated you was within your own control. If she kept acting like she was first and foremost a fiction writer, people would start to treat her that way.

This obstinacy was one reason so many of her readings

went badly. The audience felt let down, and they showed it. In some cases, people had come because they'd been told Susan was going to read from a book of essays or give a talk on a certain topic. Then, without warning, she'd pull out a story. Her stories tended to be long. Of course, she was aware—she could not help being aware—of her listeners' displeasure. How, then, she could do this—and do it repeatedly—was one of many things about her that remains a mystery to me. It made no sense. It's your work: even if you can't leave 'em laughing or in tears, why would you want to leave them pissed off?

Big changes would come. *The New Yorker* began publishing her stories, including her much-lauded 1986 story about the AIDS crisis, "The Way We Live Now," which John Updike would select as editor of *The Best American Short Stories of the Century* (1999). *The Volcano Lover* was both a best seller and a sweeping critical success. *In America* won the National Book Award for fiction. People ate their hats. I heard that after the National Book Awards ceremony, she could not stop crying.

She began to refer to herself jokingly—and not so jokingly—as a late bloomer. But, in the end, as she knew very well, her literary reputation continued to rest mainly on her best essays, and those had been written long ago.

If only she hadn't waited; if only she'd followed her heart sooner. The older she grew, the more she regretted not having devoted a far greater part of herself to art rather than to criticism—just as she regretted the strong sense of moral obligation that had driven her to spend so much time on good causes. More artist and less critic, more author and less activist: that was the way she *should* have lived. And now she saw also how she had allowed her obsession with travel to become too much of a distraction from writing.

No, she was not happy with her life's work. She had failed to reach the goals she had set for herself in her youth. True greatness had eluded her. She was like Woolf's Mr. Ramsay, stuck at Q, dreaming of Z.

But it was not all her fault. "I lost a decade," she used to say. She was talking about the decade preceding her first appearance in print. If it hadn't been for marriage and motherhood, of course she'd have published sooner. (This is somewhat confusing since, for much of that time, David was not in her care, and she spent a good part of it on her own.) But she was also talking about a certain book, *Freud: The Mind of the Moralist*, the first book to be published, in 1959, by Philip Rieff. Although her name did not appear on the cover, she was a full coauthor, she always said. In fact, she sometimes went further, claiming to have written the entire book herself, "every single word of it." I took this to be another one of her exaggerations.

(This habit of exaggeration seemed to infect those who wrote about her. Because she spoke excellent French, she was said to speak "multiple" languages and to read Mann and Benjamin in the original, though in fact she did not know German. Indeed, languages were not one of her many major passions, and she always said if she hadn't lived so much in France she probably wouldn't even speak French. Because she was such a big moviegoer, she was said to go to the movies "almost every day of the week," and because she always tried to sit up front, she was said always to sit exactly "in the third row, center"—as if, on at least some of those hundreds of days a year that she went to the movies, Susan's favorite seat might not already have been taken. She was said to have started college at fifteen rather than sixteen, her actual age at the time. Et cetera.)

In that "lost decade" she surely meant to include the time when, having divorced Philip and moved with David to New York, and having refused alimony and child support, she had to support herself and David—mostly by teaching—on her own. (Though, in fact, it was precisely during this time that she wrote *The Benefactor*.) As she put it, after serving one "prison sentence"—her childhood— she had been forced to serve two more: her marriage to Philip, and David's childhood.

A year after her first book came out, the publication, in

Partisan Review, of "Notes on 'Camp'" made her name. Another year or so, and she was internationally famous. Not bad for a woman barely into her thirties. And yet, to her, cause for shame! After all, she had received her BA at eighteen. Publishing your first novel at thirty hardly makes you a slacker, but nor is it considered precocious. And she was very bound up in this idea of herself as precocious. She tended to bring up the lost decade whenever there was a buzz about some literary or intellectual wunderkind, which roused her competitive spirit. If she'd been able to emerge upon the literary scene sooner, she would have been seen as a true prodigy and created an even bigger splash than she had done. I don't know if she always remained resentful about this, but when I knew her it was clear she felt cheated.

I broke her heart, she told me, when I wailed: "I'm twenty-five years old and I've accomplished *nothing*."

And she felt cheated in other ways. Fame was one thing; money, another. For most of her life, she felt, her work had not been fairly rewarded. She had no real financial security until she was well into her fifties. And yet, there were plenty of other writers and artists, including any number in her own circle, whose work made them money. Perhaps it was not ideal that so many of her friends and acquaintances were rich, and that she was often thrown into the company of the superrich. It sometimes seemed she was surrounded by people who had so much more than she: people who owned their own apartments (a far less common situation then than now); people who had servants; people who collected masterpieces; people who, when they traveled, always traveled first class. It galled her that, with very few exceptions, these people could not claim to be making the kind of worthy contribution to culture and society that she made. During the period right before she signed up with an agent, when she was worried about making the rent—now four or five times what she'd been paying at 340—she complained to one of her born-rich friends, who enraged her by suggesting that she think about moving out of the city. It would have been an enormous help if, during this time, she had been granted a MacArthur Fellowship (as she would be, finally, in 1990). But year after year, she saw herself passed over: nine years of bitter frustration.

As she grew older, it became increasingly hard for her to accept that she had to do anything just for the money. Earlier, she had looked down on writers with agents, writers who went on big publicity tours, who knew exactly how many copies their books had sold, and who were, to her disgust, vulgarly concerned with the size of their advances—just as earlier she had believed that a serious writer would disdain financial awards and silly prizes. Beckett—

But now she saw that, had she been a little more

concerned about money herself, she might have been spared the endless piecework and the many jobs and appearances that had taken so much of her time. And this became another regret. She should have heeded sooner the advice of those who kept telling her that, with a different attitude and the right agent, she too could be a millionaire.

Other failures ate at her. I thought that she was blessed in having managed to stay friends, in some cases for decades, with ex-lovers, and that this spoke very well for her. But about her love life she was inconsolable. And then there was her relationship with David, whom she continued to refer to, always, as "my only family." How it tormented her that they had spent so much time at odds, that there had been so many periods of strain and hostility and distance.

Once when we were together and she was pouring her heart out, I remember thinking that anyone who happened to be eavesdropping would say to himself, Now here is a poor, sad creature: lonely, unloved, and misunderstood. I remember thinking how that listener would never guess that, in fact, here was a person who was always surrounded by a large circle of people who cared, who honored and respected her, and a smaller circle of people who were constantly helping her, and within that circle a devoted group who would always be there for her, no matter what;

and that, if she didn't want to, she would not have to spend a day of her life alone.

Even people who had never met Susan sent checks to help pay the medical expenses to treat her cancer.

We are on the phone, supposedly trying to make a date. She grows sullen, impatient. "What?" I say. "Now you don't want to get together?" A big sigh. "Yes, of course I do. But not like this. Not like two society ladies arranging to have tea. We used to live together!" (Translation: I called because I need someone to be with now. Don't talk to me about next fucking Tuesday. Come now, I need someone NOW.)

Another time, she calls because she is having a problem, something to do with the recent fire in her apartment. After a brief, vaguely worded exchange, I say, "Do you want me to come over and help?" "Yes, of course, but don't you see? It's not for *me* to *ask* for your help, it's for *you*, as a friend, to *offer*." (I did offer, but not quickly enough.) She has decided to hire an assistant and she wants my advice. When I suggest a young woman whom we both know, she blows up: "I don't want some kid! I'm not looking for a typist! I need someone who knows me and knows my work and the things I care about. Oh, just forget it. Clearly, you have no idea what it means to be in my situation. It's a problem you can't relate to because it's a problem you don't have, *and you never will.*"

She was bitter. She was wrathful. She was mad at the world. A Joe Louis who wanted to hurt someone.

And in this way, too, she reminded me of my mother: she was the kind of person about whom other people say, You can't win with her.

But, to be honest, I often played dumb with Susan, and if there was one thing that could drive her insane, it was that.

———

TWICE WHILE WRITING this book, I have dreamed about her. In the first dream, we are at the ballet. We meet during intermission. She has been ill. Her hair is short, thin, dry, red. "Well," she demands, "have you infiltrated?" She means the ballet company. "For example," she says, "how tall is that dancer?" I tell her. "No, no," she says. "He's at least twenty feet tall." I tell her that's impossible. No dancer is twenty feet tall. At which she becomes agitated and says, "How can I trust you now?"

In the second dream, I am staying in her house, alone. She is away, and I have agreed to house-sit for her. While I am there, two strangers, a couple named Pat and Mike Tribe, arrive. They have come to take over the house. They are polite but firm, and though I try I am unable to stop them.

How can she trust me? I don't know how to infiltrate properly, and I allow the Tribes to invade her home.

Just as, early on, in her precocious years, she was used to being the youngest in a group, in her later years it was the reverse. This was because the older she became, the more she preferred befriending and socializing with people who were younger than she, often much younger. And it was also because she wanted to go places and do things generally associated with youth. Being the oldest person in a room did not make her self-conscious; it did not even appear to make her feel—as it probably would most people—old. The idea that she could ever be out of place anywhere because of her age was beyond her—like the idea that she could ever be de trop.

I remember how out of place I myself felt at the Bruce Springsteen concert at Madison Square Garden in August 1978: a twenty-seven-year-old among all those screaming, devastatingly young-looking kids. And I remember how strange Susan looked to me, the oldest person by far within view, her wild gray hair never so glaring, definitely catching some looks. But if she noticed any of this herself, she gave no sign. Again, I think her behavior had everything to do with her fierce determination to make up for a youth she felt had been stolen from her.

She was up for *anything*. She must do *everything*. But there were times (like at that Springsteen concert) when her enthusiasm seemed forced. She often struck me as someone who wanted to be feeling ten times what she actually felt. Ten times happier, or ten times sadder, or ten times more stimulated by whatever it was that had her attention. (Could this have been at least partly at the root of her hunger to watch so many movies and performances—to repeat every experience that gave her pleasure—such a staggering number of times? *Never enough*: what a cruel ethic to live by.)

And there were times when her obsessive curiosity, which she herself considered her biggest virtue, seemed closer to voyeurism: not a virtue.

She was *so* New York. And in her boosterism, in her energy and ambition, in her can-do, beat-whatever-the-odds spirit, in her childlike nature—and in her belief in her exceptionalism and in the power of her own will, in self-creation, and in the possibility of being reborn, the possibility of endless new chances, and of having it all—she was also the most American person I knew.

"Well, here we are," she says, huddling beside Joseph. "Not even middle-aged, and struck by the top two killer diseases."

The talk turns to *Hope Against Hope*, Nadezhda Mandelstam's memoir of life under Stalin, in which she compares that hell to the pain and suffering of normal family life: "What wouldn't we have given for such ordinary heartbreaks!" Joseph shrugs, unmoved. "Trust me, she had plenty of those, too." And, after a broody pause: "You know, in the end, none of it matters, what happens to you in life. Not suffering. Not happiness or unhappiness. Not illness. Not prison. Nothing." Now, that's European.

She liked people who were physical, who liked to touch and be touched, and who were voluble and confessional and easy to open up with—a way of being she sometimes called Jewish. And she liked terms of endearment; she herself often used "darling" and "dear." And, as much as she criticized other people to their faces, she was also quick to compliment. She flattered and talked people up all the time. She would gush about a person—loudly if there happened to be a crowd—while he or she stood by, beaming or blushing. Introducing you to someone famous, she would flatter you by saying, "Have you two already met?"

She might not consider you her equal—she considered few people her equal—but that didn't mean she didn't want to hear your life story. She didn't always have to be the center of attention. She loved to talk, but she also loved getting others to talk, the more intimately the better. It happened fairly often, she said, that someone would tell her something they claimed they had never told anyone else before. Which was interesting, given that she was known to be indiscreet, no good at keeping secrets, and, as she admitted, incapable of not betraying others' confidences.

The little ritual—copied, like so much else she did, by many of us—of spending the last few minutes before leaving on a trip searching the shelves for a book she hadn't yet read, to take along.

She traveled so much that everywhere I go she has been there before me.

David had her buried in Paris. In the same cemetery as Beckett.

I saw her drunk once. It was an accident. We had arranged to meet at the bar of a small restaurant on lower Sixth Avenue before going to the Film Forum. She had some event she had to go to right before meeting me, and there, against her custom, she'd had a drink: a margarita. She arrived at the bar already tipsy. Then she had another margarita, which she drank very quickly; I had to steady her on the way to the theater. I could tell, though, that she was too drunk to know she was drunk.

It was a strange film, a German documentary about the making of the autobahn. Almost as soon as it began, Susan fell asleep. From time to time she'd wake up and watch for a minute or so before nodding off again. No matter: she dreamed her own movie, and when the lights came on she turned to me and said, "That was terrific, wasn't it?"

———

WHILE I WAS still in school, at Columbia, I had taken a course in modern British literature with Edward Said. Whenever I mentioned him, Susan would tease, "Sounds like you've got a crush." (Although Susan and Said had probably met by this time, they had not yet become friends.) There was truth to this. A lot of students were smitten with brilliant, handsome young Professor Said.

Then, somehow—I can't remember the details, except that I had nothing to do with them—Professor Said was coming to visit!

I have never understood what happened that day. I remember that the four of us were in the living room, where there was only one comfortable chair. I remember that Said sat in that chair without taking off his coat and that he had brought an umbrella, which he placed on the floor beside the chair. And the whole time, he kept reaching down to pick up the umbrella and then immediately put it down on the floor again.

I remember that I didn't say anything, David didn't say anything, and though Susan did her best to engage him, Said didn't say much of anything, either. He sat there in his coat, nervously playing with the umbrella and not saying much, and when he did say something it was mumbled. He sat in the one comfortable chair, the only comfortable chair in the whole apartment, looking as uncomfortable as if he were sitting on nails, picking up the umbrella and putting it down again, nodding at whatever Susan said but obviously too distracted to be really listening. Of what was discussed, all I can recall is who was and who wasn't still on the faculty at Columbia, where, years before, Susan had taught, too. The entire visit, though it did not last long, was excruciating, and it was a great relief when he was gone.

And after he was gone, Susan came to find me. "Are you all right?" I shrugged. "Look," she said, "I have no idea what that was all about, but I do know how you feel, and I'm sorry." What was she talking about? "I know what it's like when you admire someone and then you see them in an unflattering light. I know it can be very painful."

We sat together for a while, smoking and talking. How many hours we used to spend like that, smoking and talking. To me it was unfathomable: the busiest, most productive person I knew, who somehow always had time for a long conversation.

"But that's what happens," she said. "You have to be prepared for that." It had happened to her a lot, she said. Once she started meeting writers and artists, it happened over and over. "I'd be so thrilled about meeting these people—my heroes! my idols!"

And over and over she would feel let down, or even betrayed. And she was so disillusioned that she'd end up regretting having met them, because now she couldn't worship them or their work anymore, at least not in the same pure way.

One of her favorite books was Balzac's *Lost Illusions*, which she insisted I must read at once.

One of her favorite films was *Tokyo Story*. "I try to go see it once a year." (In those days, if you lived in Manhattan, this could be done.)

She was shocked when I didn't love it. (I am ashamed to say, that first time, I found Ozu's masterpiece too slow.)

"But didn't you get it? What about the part, after the mother's funeral?"—and she recited an exchange that takes place between the youngest daughter and the daughter-in-law. "Oh my God!" She clutched her throat. "Didn't that make you *weep*?"

What a dumb clod I must have seemed to her. I thought of lying just to protect her. But then she waved her hand and said, "Oh, it's just because you're too young. Years from now you'll see it again, and then you'll understand." Confident.

Actually, it didn't take years. And I didn't have to see the movie again.

> *Kyoko:* Isn't life disappointing?
> *Noriko:* Yes, it is.